THE CROSS-EYED BEAR
and other children's sermons

THE CROSS-EYED BEAR

and other children's sermons

S. Lawrence Johnson

Abingdon • Nashville

THE CROSS-EYED BEAR

Copyright © 1980 by Abingdon

Second printing 1980

Library of Congress Cataloging in Publication Data

JOHNSON, SAMUEL LAWRENCE.
    The cross-eyed bear.
    SUMMARY: A collection of 47 brief sermons using incidents and
characters from many places and points in time.
    1. Children's sermons. [1. Sermons. 2. Christian life] I. Title.
    BV4315.J634   252'.53   79-24765

ISBN 0-687-09980-3

MANUFACTURED BY THE PARTHENON PRESS
NASHVILLE, TENNESSEE, UNITED STATES OF AMERICA

PREFACE

A children's sermon needs to be short. But, like a Christmas stocking overflowing with goodies to be pulled forth one after another, the sermon should be packed with information the child can enjoy and remember.

Sermons for children may be valuable instruments. They can stimulate. They can present moral, ethical, and spiritual truths in a sweet capsule. A director of a nonsectarian camp commented, "There is nothing more valuable than a volume of sermons for children to use as a thought-provoker at our camp council weekly powwows."

Certain basic things are required whether you plant a vegetable garden or a field of wheat. Soil needs to be loosened and fertilized and properly conditioned to produce a good crop. The purpose of these printed sermons is for tilling the soil of the mind of the reader or the listener. The user is urged not only to read them to children but also to make them his or her own, supplementing them with fitting personal experiences as illustrations.

As usual, I am deeply grateful to my wife, who edits all my writing, and I am thankful for the helpfulness of Jan Maddux, reference librarian at Emmet O'Neal Library, Mountain Brook, Alabama.

To

Alice

and

to all the other

beloved

members of my family

CONTENTS

THINK ABOUT IT

A very old prayer used by Indians in North America says, "O Thou Great Spirit, Maker of men, forbid that I judge any man until I have walked two moons in his moccasins."

Those words are provocative. Perhaps you will be reminded of the words of Jesus, "Judge not, that you be not judged," or, "Judge not by appearances but with right judgment." You might think of wanting something belonging to somebody else, of being envious.

You may remember Biscuit, that little white poodle who was killed by an automobile because she could not or would not learn that big gas buggies would not get out of her way. This little dog was greatly loved by her family. They missed her so much they had to find another pet to love. They bought Shichi, a little black and white dog, called a "party poodle" in the United States, but in England referred to as a "harlequin."

Constantly, members of Shichi's family are saying such things as, "Why can't you behave like Biscuit did?" "Why do you have to race around the house as if the devil was after you? Biscuit didn't." "Biscuit never took the pillows from the couch and carried them all over the house, why must you?"

If Shichi could understand the many questions, he might ask, "Who was this Biscuit, this super dog?" He might continue, "Why must you always use her as an example?" Or, in his quieter moments, he might gain courage to retort, "Well, I'm not Biscuit, I'm Shichi."

It is human nature to compare one person to another. It is natural to liken oneself to some other person and reflect on the ways in which we differ and then get all excited and bothered.

When Biscuit was alive and wanted to go outside, she would stand near the door and quickly scrape the floor with her right hind foot. There was no mistaking what she wanted. When Shichi needs to go out, he goes to find his leash, takes one end in his mouth, and drags it to his mistress. His desire is equally obvious.

When the master and mistress used to return home after having left Biscuit for some time, she would always be waiting at the top of the basement stairs leading from the garage and would excitedly bark hello. Now, when they come back after being gone a long time, they find Shichi lying on a bed, his little pompom tail beating the air, but otherwise unmoving until he has been petted. Then he'll go wild, jumping up and down, and licking the hands of his people. Two little dogs, both with differing character traits, different habits, different personalities, but both intensely affectionate and loving.

The word *covet* means to long for or earnestly desire something belonging to another. What you covet may not be good for you. Stop a moment and recall that old prayer of the Indian American. Are you certain you really want what you have been coveting?

WALLS

To protect themselves against enemies, many people who lived in ancient times built high walls surrounding their cities. Sections of original walls still remain in many places, such as London, Paris, and Oxford.

There are many references to walls in the Bible. The psalmist wrote, "Peace be within thy walls, and prosperity within thy palaces" (KJV). The writer of the book of Hebrews in the New Testament, in referring to one of the oldest stories about walls said, "By faith the walls of Jericho fell down" (KJV).

The longest wall ever built was the Great Wall of China. It was more than two thousand miles long, twenty to fifty feet high, and up to twenty-five feet thick in some places. The construction of this wall began many years ago during the reign of Shih Huang Ti. Back in those days there were no big modern machines. It had to be built entirely by hand so it took years to complete. The top of this huge structure was paved with brick set in lime forming a roadway for horsemen. You may visit the remains of this wall today.

Scotland has two interesting walls. The Hadrian, built along the northern edge of the province of Britain, is so called because it was ordered constructed by the Roman emperor Hadrian. You have heard of the pony express, which carried letters across the Western plains of the United States in early days. This idea of transportation of mail was conceived by Hadrian. He set up an empire-wide communications network similar to our pony express. Hadrian was a poet and an architect, but he is most remembered because of the wall he ordered built.

Hadrian picked Aurelius Antonius to become emperor

after his death. Because Aurelius was a gentle and just man and his reign one of the most calm in all Roman history, people referred to him as Antonius Pious. He also ordered a wall built. Just north of the remains of Hadrian's Wall you can see standing sections of Antonius' Wall. Both were built for protection.

After World War II the city of Berlin, Germany, was divided into east and west. For East Germany and Russia it was an irritating situation. During a period of twelve years about 200,000 people a month crossed from East Germany to West Germany. It was felt something had to be done to stop this migration. August 1961, the East German police started to build a wall between the divided sections of the city.

It seems the city of Jerusalem has always been surrounded by a wall; not the same wall, but many different walls. At the end of 1948, Israeli soldiers held West Jerusalem, and the Jordan troops East Jerusalem. Barbed wire and mine fields became a wall that divided the city. When the fighting ended, Israeli tanks encircled the old city and the wall came tumbling down.

Walls can either keep people out or keep people in. The word used is protection. Sometimes walls work and at other times they do not. The protective walls of early castles were thought to be indestructible. For many of them this was true until the development of gunpowder. Then, canons battered them down. Even before gunpowder, many walls gave way to siege, some by tunnels dug beneath to allow entrance.

There have been good walls and bad walls. Often boys and girls build bad walls that keep other children away from what is wholesome, clean, and beneficial. How often have you heard someone say, "I don't want to play with you"?

Many times walls are built between people because of the color of their skin. For centuries in India there has been a class of people called "untouchable." People known as Brahmans would have nothing to do with the "untouchables." A man named Mahatma Gandhi tried very hard to break down this wall. To some extent he succeeded, but the battle still continues. In the United States, in South America, and in other places of the world, high walls have been built between blacks and whites.

During the War Between the States, Stonewall Jackson was severely wounded. One of his men asked, "General, how is it that you can keep so cool, and appear so utterly insensible to danger in such a storm of shells and bullets?"

General Jackson told the captain his belief in an eternal God was a wall of security.

THE PARADISE TREE

There is much in our Christian tradition we take for granted. We have heard things and we have done things ever since we can remember that we simply do not question. We come to the season of Advent and our attitude is: well, what of it? People have always celebrated Advent. What difference does it make to me how a custom came into being?

We are told Advent begins four Sundays before Christmas. What does that mean? Twenty more shopping days? Or, I wonder what Santa Claus will bring me this year? Or, What am I going to give Jim, Mary, Mother, Dad?

Just before Christmas your mother and father get out boxes of ornaments for trimming the tree. There are also felt objects such as covers for doorknobs, stockings, a tree skirt. There are candles and lights and breakable ornaments. Part of our Christmas tradition is a Christmas tree. It may be a tall one reaching to the ceiling. It may be a short one to stand upon a table. But we feel we must have a tree. Why?

One very old story regarding the first use of the Christmas tree is of a group of monks sent by the Bishop of Rome to carry the story of Jesus to the people of the north. One cold winter night they came upon a group of people worshiping around an evergreen tree, singing and dancing. At first the monks wanted to condemn these folks. Instead, they explained to them that the conifer was a symbol of everlasting life, growing green up from the winter snow to bear witness to the everlasting Christ.

An ancient heathen feast was called the Yeule. During this twelve-day celebration, folks used to put fir trees or branches from them in their homes or gathering places to

14

decorate and signify their anticipation of the coming springtime.

An old Christian tradition was performing mystery plays in churches. These were dramas based on scriptural themes, usually centering in the life, death, and resurrection of Jesus. In these plays, the Garden of Eden was represented by a fir tree hung with apples.

Probably the Christmas tree is a combination of these two traditions. At first, the Christmas tree was hung with apples. Later, wafers of bread, like those used in celebrating Communion, were added. Then, candies and bits of pastry came to join the apples and wafers. In turn these gave way to the types of tree decorations we use today.

German people who had the Paradise Tree on display in their homes followed a custom of lighting many candles the evening of December 24. They would place the candles on little steps forming the shape of a pyramid. During the sixteenth century, candles were added to the tree itself.

The tree, the candles, all the decorations are symbolic of God's great goodness and particularly of his gift to us of the baby Jesus.

THE ALL-SEEING EYE

Anne asked, "Do you believe in God?"

Cautiously, Susan replied, "Sure, I believe in God if there is one. My mom says I should ask God to help me when I feel a need, but I've never seen God. I've never heard God. I've never felt God. So, why talk to him?"

Not long ago, there were some very brilliant men who were saying much the same thing as Susan. They proclaimed, "God is dead."

Talk like that has gone on for a long time. Each year our universe grows smaller, or our knowledge of it increases, and as we become more aware of the complexity of the world the more confused we become. As we send probes out into vast space, we find ourselves saying, "It is utterly impossible for God to know about all this!" We remember that Jesus claimed God was aware of the sparrow's fall. Suppose he were on earth today, he might say that God was aware of each virus. We think of God as having human capabilities so we are certain he would not be informed on such insignificant things.

However, over the years and out of personal experiences, many people have come to some very positive conclusions regarding the reality of God. Mr. Job, whose story is in the Old Testament, had some very hard times; still he proclaimed, "Though he slay me, yet will I trust in him" (KJV). God had proved himself to Job just as he has to many other people in recorded history.

Do you like to climb trees? When you get up high you can see way off in the distance, much farther than you can down on the ground, can't you? Pioneers in the space industry realized that vehicles lifted high above the earth would make excellent platforms from which to observe the earth. At first observations were made by men in balloons, then in airplanes, finally came the development of satellites.

It was found that vision was greater than had ever been dreamed possible. No spot on earth can escape inspection. We can study movements in snow lines and discover plant diseases in orchards before the owner realizes anything is wrong. With fantastic cameras, some using infrared rays, we have discovered copper and other mineral deposits and underground streams of water or oil.

Instruments have been sent aloft to measure solar and cosmic radiation and magnetic fields. Spacecraft have gently landed on Mars, taken pictures and samples of soil, and beamed the pictures and the analysis of the soil back to earth.

Every day satellites are in orbit around our earth carrying sensing devices and all sorts of gadgets. You cannot see them, hear them, or feel them any more than you can see, hear, or feel God; but you believe in them and what they can do, don't you?

One day a great astronomer, Professor Ormsby Mitchel, was examining a new telescope. For fun he began to look at the nearby countryside. He turned it on a hill about twelve miles away and saw his own son and some other boys stealing apples from a tree. That night at supper the professor's son announced he was not very hungry. The father laughed. "Of couse not, you're too full of apples!"

The boy was astonished. He had not heard, seen, or felt the presence of that all-seeing eye of the telescope.

WASHING YOUR FACE

Do you remember when you first washed your face? You may say you've always done it. But that's not true. For a long time your mother, father, or someone else washed it for you.

When you first started it was a ritual. You carefully filled the washbowl, took a washcloth, wet it, cautiously rubbed on soap before you gently touched it to your chin, your nose, your cheeks, your forehead.

If you cannot recall how you performed, watch your little brother or sister. You will be amused by the concern taken in this simple task.

As you have grown older, perhaps you have thought washing your face was too much of a nuisance, an unnecessay and foolish habit. Probably you stopped washing your face for a time. The first few days did not seem to make much difference. Then your face began to feel greasy. After a couple of weeks, much to your dismay, you noticed pimples appearing. Blackheads were noticeable. Certainly it could not be because you had not washed? Unhappily, but true, that was the reason.

Do you know people who jog? If you ask them, "Is it fun?" very likely they'll reply, "No, it's hard work!" They may add that when they first began jogging it was fun, but as time went on it became boring. There are very few people who really enjoy running. But what they do like are the results of the exercise so they keep it up. A person who does this regularly will tell you, "I feel so good when I've finished. If I don't jog, I feel sluggish, and I puff when I bend or when I climb."

Prospecting for gold or other precious metals is not such

a drag as it once was. With techniques developed by geologists, some of the back-breaking labor has been eliminated, but it is still work. A good experience for you would be to go to some place like Franklin, North Carolina, where you can dig for rubies and other precious stones. There are spots where you can pan for gold. You will use the same method the old-time prospectors used. You will lift up soil in the pan, shake it gently in the water. The dirt washes away, but the gold, being heavier, sinks to the bottom of the pan. In digging for precious metals, modern seekers use sensitive instruments to learn the composition of the earth, then bring in big machines to dig. It is not such heavy work as digging with shovels, but it is still a task.

Boys and girls sometimes say they do not want to attend church because they do not get anything out of it. Psychologists have learned that "getting something" is not what is really important, rather is what eventually happens to our thinking and behavior.

If one truly believes in and worships God there are bound to be good results. Religion is something that must be completely accepted and protected. You must have faith.

Washing your face may not seem to produce results. At least, you are not aware of any while you are in the process of washing. Attending church each Sunday may not seem worthwhile while you are sitting in the pew. Much of what goes on in church may appear meaningless, but if you stop attending, you will be conscious that something important is missing from your life.

TIN SOLDIERS

Andy Foulks has a collection of miniature cars and trucks. He started gathering them when he lived in London, England, where his father was doing his internship. When he is is not using the autos to play games, he stores them in little cases.

Over the centuries boys and girls have collected and played with toys. Archaeologists, digging in the ruins of long-forgotten cities, have found dolls. They have found them buried in ancient tombs of boys and girls.

Children, rich or poor, love toys. Some toys belonging to royal children have cost fortunes. When Louis XV was a small boy he had a complete little theater with five sets of scenery. In 1750, the young heir to the throne of France was given an army consisting of thirty detachments of tin soldiers, which were very expensive. The court painter himself painted some of these puppets.

The very first toy soldier convention was held in Southampton, England, in 1950. Over ten thousand lead, tin, and plastic soldiers enacted battles from the War of the Roses, the Boer War, and other wars. There have been many protests both in the United Kingdom and the United States against allowing children to play with tin soldiers. In fact, Mrs. Anne Kerr tried to get a law through the House of Commons in England banning their use.

But there has long been considerable fascination with tin soldiers. In the sixteenth century, mock warfare was very popular among children. The art of jousting was taught with models. Wheeled miniature knights on horseback were manipulated with strings. In Munich there is a museum displaying excellent figures of knights. Blenheim

Palace near Oxford, England, has a marvelous assembly of over seven hundred figures created by a designer named Lucotte. The exhibit is placed in a beautiful cabinet mirrored to show the back of the characters. It is enchanting to view and seems to double the size of the little army.

The most elaborate army of lead soldiers was invented in 1650 for the boy Louis XIV. Two talented artists worked on them. George Chassel created the patterns. A man named Merlin executed them in silver.

About 1775 Johann Gottfried Hilpert, who had learned metalcraft from his father, had a very brisk trade in lead soldiers in Nuremburg. He was the person who established what was considered the standard height for these little men: thirty millimeters.

Undoubtedly you have eaten chocolate Easter bunnies that were hollow inside. The next time you have one think of an Englishman named William Brittain who introduced the technique for making hollow tin soldiers. He gained fame, for these were lighter weight and easier to play with and handle. Chocolate makers took up the idea for it saved them money.

In 1776 British soldiers wore red coats. In 1848 members of the Zurich infantry regiment wore tall hats with plumes. Their uniform pants had stripes down the sides. In 1914 German soldiers wore helmets with tall spikes. All soldiers of a given period seem to look alike.

Boys and girls can very easily become like tin soldiers. They want to wear clothing that duplicates that of their peers. They do not move unless someone moves them. They have fixed attitudes and behavior.

Men and women can also act like tin soldiers. For thirty years a keeper of a lighthouse had become accustomed to a loud blast of the horn going off every five minutes, night and day. While he was asleep one night something happened to prevent the horn from sounding. The lack of the noise awakened the keeper, and he cried, "What was that?"

THE CHURCH OF HEAVENLY REST

Mr. Gene Hickman is a master watchmaker, not just a repairman, but a true artist. Asked how many parts were in a good watch, he responded, "The average good watch contains about one hundred fifty parts, counting the screws, for if one is loose your watch may not keep time."

Mr. Williams is minister of a church. He is like the captain of a ship. It is his duty to oversee the total work of the institution and to know every man, woman, and child who is in any way connected to it.

Mr. Perry, Mr. Wilson, Mr. Harris, Mr. Davis, and Mr. Richards are handy with tools and understand machinery. When a new hot water heater is needed in the church building or the parsonage, they can do the job. They also assume the responsibility of maintaining the grounds.

Mrs. Martin serves as president of the Women's Fellowship. There are several women who help her by serving as heads of committees. When people in the church are ill and need transportation to the doctor or hospital, they can telephone Mrs. Evans or Mrs. Bateman and either of them or someone they appoint will drive.

Mr. Cornwell acts as superintendent of the church school and correlates this important work, integrating the program and directing the efforts of a whole group of teachers. Mr. Anderson, as chairman of the ushers, has readied a group to assume duty in that capacity at services each week.

Should Mr. Williams be called from the city or become ill, Dr. Bradford or the Reverend Mr. Baker, or any one of a half dozen men or women are willing and waiting to be asked to pinch-hit.

Corinth, the Roman capital of the province of Achaia, was located at the end of a narrow isthmus connecting continental Europe with the Peloponnesus. If you look at a map of Greece you will find this spot at the southern end of the country. A church was established there by the apostle Paul and some of his colleagues. The members were mostly Gentile Christians who were disagreeing with one another. But, in spite of the dissensions, the church flourished. Paul wrote several letters to these people. We speak of the two collections which have been preserved for us in our Bible as First and Second Corinthians. Paul made two suggestive comments to the group: "The body is not one member, but many," and "God has tempered the body together."

God gave you two eyes, two ears, two kidneys, two lungs, two hands, two feet. You can get along without one eye, one ear, one kidney, one lung, one hand, or one foot, but you will not be as efficient as if you had both members.

Paul said, "Your bodies are members of Christ!" With regard to a watch, Mr. Hickman said, "Remember, you have to have just the right amount of oil. If you have too much the works will not behave properly. Too much oil is as bad as too little."

An ordinary watch repairman can take apart a watch, clean it, and if there is a broken part, try to get a replacement. But Mr. Hickman can build a new part to take the place of the broken one. As minister of the church, Mr. Williams does his work in a similar way. If Mrs. Simmons feels she can no longer act as treasurer of the church, Mr. Williams must be ready with suggestions of other capable people who might be willing to assume the responsibility.

The church can function without you. It may appear to operate very well. But it will work better if you are doing your part. What is your part? It may be acting as a leader; it may be serving as a dedicated follower.

A story is told about Dr. Stephen Tyng, one-time minister of an Episcopal church in New York. One day a man said, "Dr. Tyng, I want to become a member of this church."

"What particular duty do you want to assume in the church? Do you want to teach in the church school? Would you like to train to become a member of the vestry? Or, would you rather just attend services and contribute generously of your monies?"

"I'm not really interested in any of the things you've mentioned. I just want to join the church."

The good doctor replied, "Then it's not this church you want to join. What you want is the church of the heavenly rest."

BORROWED PLUMAGE

Do you remember the story of how Tom Sawyer got the neighborhood boys to paint a fence for him? He made them believe it was fun.

Why do people paint things? Painting could be to preserve something. It might be to make an object look better or to cover up dirt. Possibly it could make something like a road sign more legible.

Painting can be hard work, but it can also be fun. You have to approach the project in the right frame of mind. Tom persuaded his companions that it was not hard work, and they got the job done.

Before the time of Jesus, there was a slave in Athens named Aesop. We know almost nothing about him, but he was probably highly educated as were many of the slaves in his day. Aesop told lots of stories that we call fables.

In one of his fables, Aesop said that Jupiter once announced he was going to appoint a king over the birds. He wanted every single bird to appear before him, so he could choose the most beautiful.

All the birds went to the bank of a stream and began washing and preening their feathers. Among these birds was a jackdaw who knew he was very ugly. However, he was determined to try to fool the god and become king. He waited until all the other birds had left. Then he picked up the most gaudy of the feathers that had been dropped and fastened them to his own body. No more colorful sight paraded before Jupiter. Just as the god was ready to crown the jackdaw king, the other birds stripped him of his borrowed plumage.

Things are not always what they appear to be. At times a

coat of paint can cover a broken piece of wood, making it seem to be in perfect condition. The feathers made the jackdaw different. You know the children in your neighborhood pretty well, just as you know your schoolmates. You may know some boys and girls who appear to be nice, worthwhile, clean, and good when, in fact, they are untrustworthy, unhelpful, unclean, and unkind. They will tell lies, cheat, be discourteous, mock and torment others; but to the adults around them they present a different personality.

Your classmates and the boys and girls in your neighborhood know about you, too. They know if you have covered your real feathers and preened to be something you are not.

In *The Merchant of Venice*, Shakespeare wrote, "All that glisters is not gold."

A FRIEND IN NEED

Everybody needs friends. Some of us need only people friends. Others of us need animal friends as well.

All of us should also make friends with books. One serious problem facing the world today is that many boys and girls are growing up without being able to read or write properly.

When your mothers and daddies and grandparents were young they were taught to memorize poems or passages of books that appealed to them or that were assigned to them by their teachers. These pieces of prose or verse proved to be good friends through the rest of their lives. During the last war, prisoners who were not allowed contact with any other humans say they would have gone mad had they not been able to quote to themselves from the Bible and other books.

The book of Judges contains stories just as good as any suspense tales ever written. In the eleventh chapter you can read about a fellow named Jephthah. He was a son of an unlawful wife. The legitimate sons thought they were completely within their rights in driving Jephthah out of their home. Jephthah was a man of particular skills. The time came when the brothers would need his help and friendship.

A wise boy or girl, man or woman, will always try to keep friendship alive and cultivate new ones. It is a foolish person who will let friendship slip away through neglect or because of a misunderstanding. Being human, all of us get our feelings hurt once in a while, but we should never let the hurt destroy our friendships.

The Greek philosopher, Aristotle, asked, "What is a friend?" He responded to his own question, "A single soul dwelling in two bodies."

Friendship should be among the most prized of life's possessions. They are worth far more than money and lands. The late Associate Justice Lamarr of the United States Supreme Court wrote in his will, "The testator leaves to his family his friendships, many and numerous in hope they will be cherished and continued."

A rabbi with a sense of humor was telling about a letter he had received from his son, "Dear Dad: I'm in Chicago, broke, and have no friends. What shall I do?" By return mail, Rabbi Fine answered, "Dear Abe: Make some friends quickly." Later the rabbi sent his son money, but he let him worry for a day first.

Many people do not take an active part in any church. In times of distress the church can be a great friend. Had Abe paid a little more attention to the synagogue when he arrived in Chicago he would have had some friends.

The best friends are not always those who are the wealthiest or who have the most impressive jobs. It is a great mistake to cultivate a friendship with someone just because he is popular, or a good athlete, or good looking. There is nothing wrong with having friends like that, but it is foolish to go out of your way to make such a friend.

His brothers had thrown Jephthah out of the house. Later, when they invited him to assume leadership because they recognized his sterling qualities, Jephthah was a bit doubtful. Wouldn't you have been? But, he reacted as a true friend. He put aside his hurt and accepted.

Right now your friends surround you everyday. As you get older, you may not see them as often, but it seems that when you need one, a friend will turn up as if in answer to your call. Having made friends, remember that you are a friend. It is up to you to be on hand when you are needed. True friendship is generous, unselfish, and forgiving.

FEAR

Many years ago, people in the town of Salem, Massachusetts, were afraid of witchcraft. Some young girls began acting very strangely. They blamed their odd behavior on certain folks whom they called "witches."

The Crucible tells about events at that time. Arthur Miller, who wrote the play, suggested that the happenings came about because the girls had eaten something containing a substance that acted like LSD. The girls did not understand what was happening to them, nor did anyone else. This lack of understanding bred fear. The results of this fear ended with the death of several people.

If Mr. Miller's theory is correct, and there is little to discredit it, the knowledge of such a substance was not new. This same thing has occurred many times during history. As you grow older, you will someday enjoy reading a very exciting story by John Fuller, "The Day of St. Anthony's Fire." This story tells about a substance called ergot that unknowingly was in the flour used in bakeries in a small French town. People who ate bread baked with this ergot-infested flour began hallucinating. Dozens of them went mad, screaming with fear. Some died.

Ergot is a mold found on grain, which may be a deadly poison. A tiny amount can cause a person to go insane for hours. Sometimes a person who had suffered and appeared to be recovered would again hallucinate weeks or even months later.

Fear of the unknown can be just as dreadful as fear of something known. Mrs. Frank Bellamy of New Orleans, Louisiana, became frightfully sick to her stomach. She was rushed to the hospital and put through a series of tests, but doctors were unable to discover the cause of her distress.

Mr. Bellamy is a sailor. At the time he was on a voyage in the Mediterranean. Mrs. Bellamy had read in the newspaper that there was a dreadful storm in the sea just south of Marseilles. She became convinced her husband's ship had been caught in that storm and had sunk. Mr. Bellamy had often told his wife of the many ships wrecked in such storms. Her fear was so intense that she became physically ill. As soon as she learned her husband was all right she recovered.

In the early 1650s, people in the village of Hampton, New Hampshire, were afraid to walk along the roads at night, because they might be followed by a ghost riding a broomstick. Two young men were drowned in the Hampton River when their boat capsized. People accused "Goody" Cole of having powers that she used to upset the boat. "Goody" Cole was tried in the county court of Norfolk in 1656. Thomas Philbrick testified that his calves could not eat grass, because Mrs. Cole had placed a curse on them. Goodwife Moulton and Goodwife Sleeper declared under oath that while they were talking with "Goody" Cole, they had heard something scraping against the boards of the window, but when they looked, nothing was there. Such evidence was conclusive.

Mrs. Cole was sentenced to be whipped and imprisoned for life. For fifteen years she remained in jail before being released. Almost immediately she was rearrested and charged with witchcraft. The record of the court reads: "Mrs. Cole, now a prisoner at the bar is not legally guilty, but there was a suspicion she was familiar with the devil."

What was the truth about Mrs. Cole? No one knew then. We do not know now. We do know that people were afraid, and fear of the unknown caused dreadful things to happen.

Long ago, the prophet Isaiah wrote, "I will trust, and not be afraid: for the Lord Jehovah is my strength and my song," (KJV). The author of First John said, "There is no fear in love; but perfect love casteth out fear" (KJV).

DEEP WATER

"Water, water, everywhere, nor any drop to drink," said the Ancient Mariner, according to Samuel Taylor Coleridge.

For hundreds of years Bristol, England, has been an interesting port city. It was from Bristol that John Cabot sailed in the *Matthew* in 1497. After discovering Newfoundland, he sailed down part of the coastline of North America. Some historians maintain that the Americas were named in honor of Richard Amerycke, one-time sheriff of Bristol, and a friend of Cabot.

In the center of Bristol stands the lovely Lord Mayor's Chapel, the only church in England owned by a corporation. An English corporation is like a city council in the United States.

A church owned by a city, not just a specifically organized religious group? Yes. Churches have been owned by towns, cities, or state governments. Such was the case in Wakefield, New Hampshire, when, in 1884, the town called the Reverend Asa Piper to come as its minister.

When Wakefield was founded, the area was divided into sections of one hundred acres each. It was designated that one of these "shares" was to be given to the first settled town minister and that a second one hundred acres be set aside for the purpose of supporting the work of this minister. This land was wilderness. It could only be used for farming after lots of labor, hard labor.

Some of Mr. Piper's land bordered on what was known as Lovell's Pond, today called Lovell Lake. In the lake are three islands: one tiny, one medium-sized, one large. The biggest has always been known as the Great Island. Mr.

Piper was given title to the Great Island. He was convinced it would be an excellent place to pasture his sheep. Mr. Piper did not own a boat, but his neighbor did. Mr. Piper hired his neighbor to ferry the animals to the island.

The man took over a load and quickly returned for a second batch of sheep. After the third group of sheep he did not come back to the mainland for a long time. When he finally rowed over, he still had the sheep in his boat. He told Mr. Piper, "I've been all over that island, from one end to the other, and there isn't a mite of water on it. Sheep have to drink, don't they? So I've brought the critters back."

How often have you said, "I've nothing to do"? There are libraries full of good books and records. You could do many helpful things aound the house if you wanted to do something. What you are really saying is that you do not want to put forth any effort; that you want someone to entertain you.

Beth was asked to help with vacation Bible school at Grace Church. She was told she would be given a small amount of money, and she could go on the Friday outings to the lake. Beth was an excellent swimmer, but she would not take the job. However, during the entire six weeks the vacation Bible school was in session she was heard complaining to everyone that she had nothing to do.

Uncle Charles offered his nephew Jimmy money for train fare from Marblehead into Boston to attend concerts on the Esplanade. Jimmy refused. Each evening when he could have been in Boston enjoying music, he sat on his porch telling all who passed by that he had nothing to do.

Be assured the sheep could see the water of the lake all around the island. Many of us, like Mr. Piper's neighbor, or Beth, or Jimmy, with water, water all around us, still cannot see a drop to drink.

JUST LIKE THAT

Physicians are constantly cautioning us to wash our hands. They say we may catch more diseases by not washing our hands than by any other way. So, do not mention this to your parents, but something wonderful once happened because a man forgot, or just did not take the time to wash his hands.

One day in 1879, Dr. C. Fahlberg of Johns Hopkins University was eating a piece of bread. He noticed it had a distinctly sweet taste. At first he was at a loss to understand why. Then he remembered he had not washed his hands when he left his laboratory.

He returned to his lab and carefully studied everything he had touched during the morning. He discovered an intensely sweet white crystalline powder, saccharin. In the years following that event this substance has been a great help to many people who are on sugar-free diets.

In 1903, Edouard Benedictus carelessly knocked a glass bottle from a shelf. Picking it up, he was astonished to see that, although the flask was badly cracked, it still held its original shape. He called a friend. Together they laughed at the impossible thing that had taken place. Even though Benedictus thought it was funny, he felt there must be some reason why the glass had not completely shattered. He recalled that a solution of nitrocellulose had been in the flask. The solvent had completely evaporated. He made a note of the happening and forgot about it.

Some time later he read a story about a lovely young girl who had been badly cut by flying glass in an automobile accident. He was upset.

A few weeks later, there was a similar account of yet

another accident in which a boy was almost shredded by broken glass. Suddenly, he remembered the cracked flask. He dashed out of the house, ran to his lab, and concentrated on the practical possibilities of what he had seen. For nine hours he sat holding a flask. By morning, all was clear to him. He knew, step by step, the process he must follow. With the aid of an old letterpress and two sheets of glass, he produced what we now call shatterproof glass. He named his invention Tri-plex and received his first patent in France in 1909. The next time you are riding in a car think about Mr. Benedictus.

One day, a surveyor working in the Sudbury district of Ontario, Canada, was puzzled by the action of his compass. It was deflected ten degrees from normal. He wondered how he could finish his surveying if he could not depend on his compass. To himself he said, "I've got to find out what this is all about." In his seeking he came across the world's largest deposit of nickel. Nickel is magnetic until it has been heated to 340°-350° C. This natural magnetic quality was the reason for the deviation of the compass.

A man named Daguerre became famous in Europe for what he called dioramas, an unusual version of presenting a painted panorama. He met a physicist named Niepce who had developed a simple form of photography. Niepce discovered that silver iodide was light sensitive. Daguerre struggled for six years to find a way of making silver iodide accept a permanent image.

One day he discovered that some silver plates, which had been exposed for several weeks in a cupboard, showed permanent positive pictures. Certain chemicals were kept on the shelves. Daguerre then had to learn which one of these stored chemicals worked on the silver plate to make the pictures. He persisted until he knew the answer.

Pictures produced by the method developed by this man are known as daguerreotypes.

A long time ago, Jesus said that a boy or girl who has ears to hear should use them; that if they have eyes to see they should look. Evidence of God is all around you. Are you aware of the hand of God in what is happening?

Each day, the sun comes up in the morning and falls behind the horizon in the evening. The flowers bloom in the spring. The birds fly south in the fall. Can these things help you find God?

GREAT BIG TONGUE

Not so very long ago, your baby teeth came out, preparing the way for your permanent ones. Do you recall the antics of your tongue at the time? It kept pushing itself into the vacant spaces.

As a person grows older, sometimes a hairline crack develops in a tooth, weakening it. Suddenly, one day, a piece of the tooth breaks off, leaving a rough edge. Maybe your mother or father or one of your grandparents has had this to happen and will tell you of the experience. The tongue would keep darting over to that jagged edge and rub against it. Yes, it scratched the tongue and hurt it. But the tongue would not stop. Finally, the tongue would begin to bleed. Would that make it stop? No, it would keep right on until the dentist had a chance to fix that tooth.

Dr. Ben Smith, a Birmingham dentist, says, "It seems as if the tongue is the only part of the body that isn't connected with the brain. It's hard to control."

It is just as hard to control the tongue from speaking the wrong thing or speaking at the wrong time. There are expressions we use sometimes that may offend other people.

Mr. and Mrs. Don Coleman were on a freighter traveling in the south Atlantic. Mr. Coleman likes soup. In fact, he is overly enthusiastic about soup. The chef on this ship produced delicious soups. One noon, the Negro messman brought down an extra bowl of soup without being asked. Gleefully, Don exclaimed, "Atta boy!" This is an expression Don has used ever since he was a young child to show great approval and appreciation. Much to his surprise and chagrin, the black man was very upset, saying, "Don't you ever dare say that again. I'm not your boy!"

Wap, dago, chink, jap, honkey, and ever so many more words are degrading. We must learn to control our tongues.

In the West Point chapel are a number of shields carved in marble. They represent generals in the American War for Independence from Great Britain. One shield has no name. It is marked: Major General . . . and a birth date is given. This represents Benedict Arnold who denied his country. As you study his story, you may conclude he was justified in what he did. Some of his countrymen had given him a hard time. But, he had a trust to keep. Regardless of personal reasons, he should have controlled his tongue.

After Jesus had been arrested, some of his disciples followed the arresting party. Peter was there, and he was scared. He went over to a little pot filled with burning charcoal to warm his hands. He wished he had not come. He thought if he kept quiet he would not be noticed. But, someone recognized him and said, "You must be one of them. You, too, are a Galilean."

Peter could not control his tongue. He began to babble, "Who, Jesus? One of his followers? I never saw him before!"

The apostle Paul wrote, "Whoever loves life and would see good days must restrain his tongue from evil" (NEB).

FIRST COMES FIRST

The great prophet Isaiah heard God say, "I form the light, and create darkness: I make peace, and create evil; I the Lord do all these things" (KJV).

Do you know what "Teflon" is? Why, it's polytetrafluoroethylene, of course. But, what is that? It is used to coat the inside of pans, particularly frying pans, so food won't stick.

"Teflon" was discovered almost by accident by Dr. Roy Plunkett while he was working on refrigerants at DuPont Company about 1938. It is very slippery. The idea of using it to coat cooking utensils seems to have come to a number of people almost simultaneously around 1950.

But God was way ahead of Dr. Plunkett. It was God who, almost at the beginning of time, created soapstone. It has the qualities of Teflon when used as a cooking surface. You can have no better pancakes than those baked on a flat piece of soapstone. And, they don't stick!

Radar and sonar were developed after years of research. Radar detects by hurling radio waves at a target and having them bounce back, thus revealing the presence of airplanes, ships, or storms. Sonar does the same thing underwater by bouncing high-frequency vibrations, which are reflected back, telling of the presence of submarines or underwater mines.

Long before radar and sonar, God created the bat. You may have heard the term "blind as a bat." You might believe the bat is really blind. But it isn't. It can see, but it has very poor eyesight. It relies on its ability to send out ultrasonic squeaks, about thirty a second, which are reflected back to keep him from bumping into walls or trees. Tiny muscles deafen the ears of the bat at the instant of the squeak, then quickly relax to permit his hearing the echo. Bats have had this skill for fifty million years.

Whales and dolphins use sonar to locate objects under the water and to avoid them. There is a performing dolphin who, with eyes covered, retrieves balls to show this natural talent.

Recently, military scientists have developed heat sensors to be used on rockets to guide to their objectives. This was a remarkable discovery. But, an emerald tree boa, which lived almost nine years in the Birmingham, Alabama, Zoo, had deep pits in its lips that were heat sensitive, enabling the snake to capture its prey in total darkness.

To prevent your getting diseases, a doctor or nurse will give you an injection. How wonderful it was when the medical profession learned to introduce protective substances directly into our muscles or bloodstreams with a hypodermic needle. But, God taught the rattlesnake to use a hypodermic needle centuries upon centuries ago.

Early humans were nomadic. One of the earliest inventions leading to civilization as we know it, is ownership of land by individuals. But, territorial rights were established by the mockingbird, the squirrel, the Grant's gazelle, and other forms of animal life from the beginning of time.

With land ownership came the invention of agriculture. But the pika, a small rabbit-like animal with rounded ears and no visible tail, has always known how to harvest and store food. He carefully gathers and cures hay and stores it under overhanging rocks. Primitive agriculture is also carried on by various types of ants. Into their burrows, working ants carry leaves. Other ants chew these leaves into fertilizer and humus for gardens of mushrooms.

Today, we have jet propulsion. It was not invented by

man. God gave this method of locomotion to the squid very early in the history of the world.

Thousands of years ago, people learned how to make paper. But, God had shown the wasp long before that how to make it.

Certain insects and many marine animals use a type of electricity that is still not understood by humans. Someday, God will reveal that secret to us.

TIME TO BE LITTLE

You often use the word, but what do you mean when you say something or somebody is *little?*

The dictionary tells us little is the opposite of big, large, or great and refers to being small or being short in duration, small in quality, quantity, or degree.

When we say a boy or a girl is little we may be visualizing different things. One of you might be seeing a person who is short and thin. Another of you might be thinking of someone who has never grown up mentally or emotionally.

In a northern city live two sisters and their brother. They are middle-aged now. When they were in grade school they never would make friends with their classmates. They attended church but would never take part in any church activities. After they graduated from high school, all three of them stayed home, as they said, to take care of their parents. They could never go anywhere or do anything because they were needed at home, they said. The father died. Then, they could never do anything because they could not leave their mother alone.

After the mother died, you would have thought they could have started associating with others. But they did not. The girls said, "Brother is not very strong, you know, so we must take care of him." Actually, brother is very strong, but he has no work. He sits in the yard all summer and in the house all winter.

One of the girls developed a skin condition. She frankly admits the reason the dermatologist has not been able to clear up her problem is because it is psychosomatic. That means it is in her mind.

All three of these people are still little. They have never grown up. Probably they never will. This is a shame, because each of them has talents that could have been used to make others happy.

Take the word *little*. Put the word *be* in front of it as a prefix. It makes the word *belittle*, which means to depreciate, to minimize, to show we think someone is not worth much. It is not nice to belittle anyone. It hurts him. It could break his spirit completely. If someone belittled you, you would not be too pleased, would you?

Jesus said that if someone hits us, we should turn the other cheek. If someone is mean to you, your first reaction is to be nasty in return. Instead, try being nice. That is turning the other cheek. It works. Being mean back to someone is the little way to react. Being nice is the grown-up way.

There is a time to be little. There is a time to be grown-up. There is never a time to belittle oneself or another.

KEEP YOUR EYE ON THE BALL

There are numerous things people do for amusement. Many of them are grouped under the classification of games. There are games of chance and games of skill. Usually, each gives momentary pleasure or pain. Sometimes we try to forget what we have done in a game as quickly as possible. At other times, we will talk about the results over and over again.

Games of skill can include kicking, throwing, or knocking balls in various ways. There are several types of football games; the American football, the British rugby and soccer are among the best-known.

Baseball is built around the art of hitting a ball with a piece of wood. Cricket is also a game in which players hit, or try to hit, a ball with a bit of wood. Golf is another.

In golf, as long as a person is able to keep his ball on the fairway, or the green, his game will go very well. But as soon as the ball is knocked into the rough or into the water or weeds, the player needs to have more skill and patience, but particularly he needs to have control over himself.

A golfer was making one mistake after another. In frustration, he turned to his caddy, "I guess I must be the worst golfer in the world."

The caddy answered, "Oh, no, sir. There are some who are worse, only they don't play."

Tennis is another game of hitting a ball. A little girl who was watching her first tennis match turned to her father, "Daddy, wouldn't it be easier if they took down that net?"

All through your life you are going to have times of difficulty. There will be days when you will wish for an easier way. When that happens remember this bit of verse:

You say, my son, it can't be done?
Keep your eye on the ball.
Your statement isn't true!

You mean, my son, it can be done,
But it can't be done by you.

The architect for the Episcopal Cathedral in Cleveland, Ohio, was dejected. He complained to his wife that he had sixty plans, one after the other, and not one of them had been satisfactory. He was ready to give up.

His wife said, "Why not make it sixty-one, John?"

Plan sixty-one was accepted by the building committee.

Long ago, someone wrote, "Keep your heart with all diligence, for out of it are the issues of life." Were he alive today and familiar with the game of golf, he might say, "Keep your eye on the ball, pick the right clubs, keep trying, and you'll get the ball into the cup."

HIDDEN LANGUAGE

Modern groups, such as fraternities and lodges, use secret handshakes and symbolic gestures. When the early Christians in Rome were being persecuted, they developed a secret language of symbols that are still visible in our churches today. For example, through the centuries the fish has stood for Jesus.

Under the city of Rome, in tunnels called catacombs, the dead were buried. To avoid detection, Christians met for worship in these catacombs. They covered the walls of many of the galleries with symbolic pictures.

Each of the immediate followers of Jesus has a particular symbol. Some are: Peter, crossed keys; Andrew, a cross that looks like an X; James, a scallop shell; Philip, a cross and two loaves of bread; Thaddeus, a ship with full sail; Thomas, a carpenter's square and a spear; Bartholomew, three knives; Simon, a fish on a hook; Matthias, an open Bible and a double-bladed battle-ax.

A sacred language known by most church people is called the language of liturgical colors. As the year changes, the hangings in front of the altar, pulpit, and lectern and the stoles which the priest or minister wears are changed.

Green is the most common color. This speaks to us of trees and grass, represents nature and life, and is used after Epiphany, which comes in January, and again at Pentecost, which is about fifty days after Easter. Thus, it is used at the time of the visit of the Wise Men and again when the Holy Spirit descended on the apostles.

White symbolizes purity, light, truth, and beauty. It is used in those seasons of the year particularly relating to

Jesus: Christmas, Easter, and Epiphany. Epiphany calls to our minds the introduction of the spirit of Christ to the Gentiles. White is also used for weddings, baptisms, confirmations, and the ordinations of priests or ministers. Some churches also use white for services of Communion.

Violet suggests to us that we need to be sorry for the things we have done that we should not have done, and the things we have not done we know we should have done. It is to remind us that repentance is necessary, that we need to completely turn around.

Red calls to our attention all those who have given their lives in order that we might have our faith. It speaks of the spirit of good, the spirit of Christ, that can be in each one of us if we want it.

Sometimes boys and girls talk with God in special ways. We know that God will understand whatever we say even if people do not. God listens not only to our words but also to our inmost thoughts.

WORK, FOR THE NIGHT IS COMING

When you are young it is very difficult for you to think that life is short. Sometimes each day seems to stretch out as if it were going to last forever. You cannot understand your parents when they comment, "Goodness, here it is only two months until Christmas, and last Christmas was only a few weeks ago."

Prophet is the name given to a very wise person who is able, because of extraordinary insight, ability, or understanding, which is God-given, to explain current events and indicate what can happen because of them.

Some of the people who wrote the psalms were prophets. One wrote the Ninetieth Psalm. A pretty good guess is that it may have been written between five and six hundred years before the birth of Jesus. The psalm proclaims that God is our home base, the beginning of all life, where the game starts, and where it finishes. This wonderful poem sings, "in the morning (life) flourishes and grows; in the evening (a little time later) it dies."

Another psalmist wrote, "As for man, his days are as grass." You know grass grows up nice and fresh and green in the spring, but with the coming of fall and winter, it turns brown and lifeless.

Dr. Richard C. Bates, a doctor in Lansing, Michigan, is not only a good doctor, but also a fine lecturer with a real sense of humor. Dr. Bates asserts that a rat is old at three years, a dog at fifteen, a lion at twenty, a monkey at forty, and an elephant at fifty. He says a human is old at eighty.

Sound pretty grim, don't they, those words of the psalmist and the observations of the modern medical man? But, not so dim if you approach what has been said with the right frame of mind. Life is short, although it does not seem so when you are ten or twelve. But, ask your grandparents how they feel about it.

How then should a young boy or girl approach life?

A nine-year-old tennis champion interviewed on television was asked, "How long would a person who wanted to be good at tennis have to practice?"

The boy replied, "A kid my age needs to practice at least two and a half hours each day, every day of the week. When he gets older he needs to give more time to it."

Stephan Tieszen is a young man who is a very good violinist. In order for him to have achieved his present proficiency it has been necessary for him to spend many hours working with his instrument. There are only so many hours in life, and he has to schedule those God has given to him if he hopes to reach his desired goal of excellence during his lifetime.

Annie Walker Coghill was the daughter of a civil engineer who helped construct the Grand Trunk Railway in Canada. As a child, Mrs. Coghill observed that if something was to be accomplished it was necessary to be aware of the passage of time. Later, she wrote a gospel song:

> Work, for the night is coming;
>   Work through the morning hours;
> Work while the dew is sparkling;
>   Work 'mid springing flowers;
> Work when the day grows brighter;
>   Work in the glowing sun;
> Work, for the night is coming,
>   When man's work is done.

THE ANIMAL NOSE

This little piggy went to market,
This little piggy stayed home,
This little piggy had roast beef,
This little piggy had none!

Pigs are nice when they are little, but when they get grown we think of them as being dirty. Really, they are not. It is only when humans keep them in filthy conditions that they cannot keep themselves clean. A pig would much rather have clean water than a mud hole in which to wash himself.

What is a truffle? It is a fungus, something like a mushroom, but a mushroom grows above ground and a truffle grows underground. We know truffles were used two thousand years ago by Roman cooks. In France, chefs call them "the jewel of French cooking."

Some truffles are about the size of a common bean, others as large as an Idaho potato. Most truffles are black, but there are some in Italy that are white. These Italian ones are almost twice as expensive as the black ones, which are found in an area of southwestern France between Perigord and Cahors.

Usually truffles are found among the roots of an oak tree, called a truffle oak, naturally. They grow two to fifteen inches deep. How they are seeded or how they come to grow no one knows. Scientists have tried to learn. If truffles could be cultivated, it would be wonderful. Now they are so rare they are sometimes referred to as black diamonds.

Farmers can often tell where to look for truffles because grasses, herbs, and flowers disapper from the earth above them. But it takes lots of digging to locate them, so specially trained pigs are used to seek them out. God has given pigs a particular sense of smell.

There are an estimated forty-seven million dogs in the United States of America. Throughout the rest of the world there are millions more. It is thought the dog is the only animal that prefers human companionship to companionship of his own kind. There are one hundred twenty-two breeds of purebred dogs and an infinitive number of what can be termed never-suches, or the Heinz 57 varieties.

Dogs are probably descended from an animal which has been given the name Tomarctus. It likely looked much as a modern wolf, with a low body, thick coat, and a long furry tail. We are not sure when dogs first became domesticated. About eight thousand years ago Egyptians had dogs something like the greyhounds of today. They trained them to hunt antelope.

Dogs have one common gift, that of smell. Smell is a most important basic sense. It is a sort of communications system. Odors are smelled when molecules of gas released from some substance stimulate certain cells in the nose. Nerve impulses travel from the nose to the brain which in turn translates these impulses into information about the odor. Often a smell seems to trigger our memory about some past experience.

A sense of smell helps animals recognize their own territory, and other animals of their own kind. It is your smell that enables your puppy to recognize you. A German shepherd has 225,000 sensory cells in its nose.

Ancient folklore tells of a dog that recognized his master after they had been separated for many years just by the master's smell. Veterinarian Dr. Allen Price tells of a hound belonging to a friend in Montana. It followed a fourteen-day-old trail for seventy-six miles. In an article in *Science Digest*, Dr. O. Chapman says, "Through foot odor of a man pressed out through his shoes and clinging to faint footprints, a dog can, in effect, see an unknown or a known person."

What particular gifts has God given you?

WASTE NOT, WANT NOT

Waste not, want not, is a maxim I would teach.
  Let your watchword be dispatch, and practice
      what you preach;
Do not let your chances like sunbeams pass you by,
  For you never miss the water till the well
      runs dry.

Rowland Howard wrote the above lines in a poem entitled "You Never Miss the Water" in *Peterson's Magazine* in 1876.

The word *adage* means a saying which, because of constant use, has become accepted as being very valuable to our thinking.

After cottonseed has been separated from the fibers, it is taken into a mill to be examined, graded, then crushed and cooked to rupture the oil cells. After the oil has been pressed from the meats, the hulls are formed into cakes which, in turn, provide excellent fodder for cattle.

The oil can be used in several ways after it has been processed. What is to be sold as salad oil must be winterized. Oil becomes cloudy at 40 to 50 degrees. Winterizing prevents this from happening. Other oil is treated with hydrogen to make it into a firm, greasy substance which we call margarine and use in place of butter.

Many centuries ago, the Chinese developed crude methods of obtaining oil from cottonseed. They used the oil for lamps and for medicinal purposes. They fed the hulls to cattle. By the time cottonseed oil was being extracted in the United States, the value of feeding the hulls to cattle had been forgotten, so they were either thrown away or burned. About 10 percent of the seed was kept for planting the crop the next year.

In 1857, the Mississippi legislature passed a law requiring every cotton gin owner to remove or destroy all the cottonseed falling from the gin so it would not be a health hazard. Think of all the cattle that might have benefited from those burned hulls.

During World War II cottonseed hulls were used in making furfural, a chemical valuable in the production of synthetic rubber. When we wanted something, we stopped wasting.

Petroleum is a combination of two Latin words: *petra*, meaning rock; and *oleum*, signifying oil. Petroleum has been found all over the world. The largest producing wells are now in the Middle East. The most plentiful wells of the United States are in Texas, Louisiana, California, Oklahoma, and Alaska. In Canada, Alberta and Saskatchewan have the most productive wells. Much petroleum has been found along the Panuc River in Mexico. No one really knows how petroleum was formed in the earth although there are many theories.

In early times, humans were aware of petroleum that seeped to the surface of the earth. Ancient Egyptians coated their mummies with asphalt, and the Chinese used natural gas as fuel back as far as 1000 B.C. The Assyrians used asphalt to hold bricks together, and boatmen of times long past smeared reeds with it. Even today, you may see boats on the Euphrates River made in this ancient manner.

The Indians of North America used petroleum hundreds of years ago before the white man arrived. Jesuit missionaries found them using it as medicine too. But, you might say the modern oil industry as such began in Romania about 1850. Then a man named Drake drilled a well near Titusville, Pennsylvania, and on August 27, 1859, found oil at the depth of 691½ feet.

For many years, people thought the world's supply of oil was inexhaustible, and no one gave any thought to conserving it. Today, we realize our supply is limited, but we still do little to preserve it. Each year billions of gallons of crude oil are wasted. Untold numbers of gallons of gasoline are burned unnecessarily.

In the Gospel of John, we are told a story of how Jesus fed a lot of people who had gathered together to hear him speak. After they had finished eating, the Master said, "Gather up the fragments that remain, that nothing be lost" (KJV).

CLIMB UP AND LOOK DOWN

For years the Eiffel Tower in Paris was the tallest structure in the world. It was designed by Alexandre Eiffel for the Paris Exposition of 1889.

Elevators take you from platform to platform right on to the top where you may eat in one of the restaurants and look out over the city, taking in the Notre Dame Cathedral, one of the finest examples of Gothic architecture in existence. Open your eyes, and you can see the homes of the very rich and the shacks of the very poor.

Japan has a building like the Eiffel, but taller, the Tokyo Tower. It is the tallest independent steel structure in the world. You could spend an entire day viewing the Disney-like animated tableau on the ground floor, the wax museum on the third floor, and other interesting features. You can pay money and go right to the top and look out over the biggest city in the world.

The city of Birmingham, Alabama, commisioned Guiseppe Moretti, a famous Italian sculptor, to design a statue of a great iron man to represent the god Vulcan. It took seven months to complete and then was shipped to St. Louis for display at th St. Louis Fair. After that event, Vulcan stands atop Red Mountain. You can climb or take an elevator to the top of this statue and look over the famous Medical Center and be reminded not only of suffering but also of the fact that man and God together can provide healing.

Just before the hundredth anniversary of the founding of the United States some of the most important men in France met for dinner. Professor Edouard de Laboulaye said, "If only both countries together might build a monument to celebrate American independence it could bring honor to each." In the group was a famous young sculptor, Auguste Bartholdi. It was in his mind that the Statue of Liberty was born.

France built the statue, and the United States provided the base. Miss Liberty was dedicated on a cold rainy day in October, 1886. She stands on Bedloe's Island in the New York harbor. You may go almost to the top of the statue and look over the city. You will see the George Washington Bridge and lots of modern skycrapers, and be reminded that countries can work together on projects, that our country has come a long way from the time it was founded.

One day, Jesus climbed a hill at one end of the Lake of Galilee. He could look down and see the great city of Tiberius, and over to Safad, the mystical city on the mountaintop. He spoke thoughts that we call the Sermon on the Mount, telling the people they should be like the lights of the city of Safid which can be seen at night. He admonished them not to continue to be angry with one another. He advised them to love one another. From that point on high Jesus revealed many truths for those who would look and see what they observed.

GO AHEAD, TALK!

There have been many attempts to define prayer. Perhaps the best way is simply this: prayer is talking *with* God. Not talking *to* God, but talking *with* him. That means listening to his answers.

James Montgomery, the son of a Moravian minister, once was thrown into prison, because he wrote a poem commemorating the fall of the Bastille in France. Another time he went to jail for writing about a riot in Sheffield, England. When he was in prison with a lot of time to think, he put on paper the words, "Prayer is the soul's sincere desire, uttered or unexpressed."

We do not understand prayer or how it works, but it is very real. What is gravity? It is a force that keeps our feet on the ground. Without it, we would go floating off into space. But we do not really know what it is or how it works any more than we know about prayer. They are mysteries.

The late Dr. Dwight J. Bradley was a Congregational minister, often referred to as a mystic. He had many strange experiences. One cold night he was sitting at his desk in the tower of his church in Newton Center, Massachusetts. He picked up his pencil with his left hand. Now, Dr. Bradley was right-handed. Without realizing what was happening, he began to write with his left hand. When he became aware of what he had been doing, he read a beautiful poem he had jotted down. You can read that poem in an anthology of American poetry. It is entitled "The Disciples." What happened? We do not understand.

On another occasion, a parishioner called him late one night begging him to come to his house, saying his little daughter was dying. Many people were in the child's bedroom when Dr. Bradley arrived. In a firm voice, he ordered them to leave. No one questioned him. They left. Dr. Bradley fell to his knees and prayed. We do not know what he said to God or what God said to him. But we do know that he listened as well as talked.

For two hours, Dr. Bradley remained on his knees. The doctors had said only a miracle could save the girl. A miracle took place. The youngster sat up, got out of bed, went to the head of the stairs, and called down to her parents, "Please bring me something to eat. I'm hungry."

Dr. Bradley continued to talk with God. We can be certain he thanked the Heavenly Father for his great goodness.

When we pray we need to have faith that something will happen. Some years ago, a group of people gathered in a church in Tulare, South Dakota, to pray for rain. A ten-year-old girl was asked, "Susan, for heaven's sake, why are you carrying your umbrella?"

Susan answered, "I thought we came here to pray for rain."

THIS SHALL BE A SIGN

Webster's dictionary has a lot to say about signs: "A conventional symbol representing an idea; a motion or action or gesture by which a thought is expressed; a publicly displayed notice."

Often the word sign appears in our Bible. Perhaps one of the most important sentences in which the word is used is, "This shall be a sign unto you; you shall find the babe."

In the book of Judges there is a story about a man who asked for a sign of the presence of God, saying, "Behold, I will put a fleece of wool on the floor, and if the dew be on the fleece only, and it be dry upon all the earth beside, then shall I know that thou wilt save Israel by mine hand, as thou hast said" (KJV).

An interesting and fairly recent development is the use of what are known as international road signs. If you see a picture of a truck appearing to be descending a hill with a line drawn across the sign you and anyone else from any country of the world will know the meaning. No matter what language you speak, when you see a curvy line you are warned the road ahead has many turns. These international signs are quickly becoming as universal a language as music.

For centuries God has posted signs. In the New Testament, we read that Jesus said, "In the evening you say it will be fine weather for the sky is red and in the morning you say, it will be stormy today for the sky is red."

More and more these days you will notice the sign, No Smoking. It has been discovered that people who smoke can get lung cancer or problems with their hearts. One of the unfortunate aspects of smoking is that it not only affects the person who is actually smoking but all those around who must breathe the contaminated air.

Do you live in a section of the country where ice forms on a lake or stream when it gets cold? A boy named Frank went skating on the Jim River that runs through Redfield, South Dakota. Authorities had placed a sign, Thin Ice. But Frank ignored the sign. It was the following spring before his body was found.

Some folks, even though they are not artists, want to be as creative as possible. There are canvasses and canvas boards that are numbered to indicate the color of paint that should be used in certain places to create a picture. Jackie Cole was a young girl who seemed to be lacking ability to paint or draw, but she could use several of these aids. She was very happy with the outcome. Then, much to her surprise, she learned she did have artistic talent and could create her own paintings.

Jackie had followed the signs to success.

MOON CITY

Alex Haley, a black man, wrote a book entitled *Roots*. It is about his family's background and is very interesting. It took Mr. Haley years of research to find all the details necessary for learning where his ancestors came from and who they were.

All families have histories. Some people have detailed accounts dating back several hundred years and do not need to do research. They can tell you all sorts of things that happened to many of their ancestors, some good, some bad; they probably could write books as interesting as Mr. Haley's if they wished.

Cities also have histories that can make fascinating reading. Jericho is one of the oldest occupied sites in Palestine. The name Jericho probably means "moon city," suggesting that the worship of a moon god or goddess was practiced there in very early times. Over and over again you have heard the name Jericho because of events taking place there. Remember Zacchaeus who climbed a tree to see Jesus? That was in Jericho. Of course, you recall the story of the Good Samaritan, which happened on the road between Jerusalem and Jericho. And, you might know that Jesus restored the sight of Bartimaeus near the "moon city."

Archaeological finds show us that humans lived at the site of Jericho many thousand years ago. In that part of the world there have been many earthquakes. When buildings were leveled by a quake, people simply built on top of the debris. Archaeologists can dig to certain depths and find out what kind of life the people of that particular level enjoyed. It is believed that Jericho was a very wealthy city.

The many vessels of brass and iron found seem to prove this.

The children of Israel were fleeing from Egypt to the Promised Land. They came to the banks of the Jordan and stopped across the river from Jericho. General Joshua, who was at the head of the Israelite army, sent spies into the "moon city." The king of Jericho had an excellent intelligence system and immediately learned of the presence of the spies and sent police to arrest them. A woman named Rahab hid them on the roof of her house. She made the spies promise that if the Israelites were successful in their attack on the city they would spare her and her entire household.

General Joshua did not attempt to attack until he had complete knowledge of the conditions inside the city. That is what the Lord told him to do. Jericho was known as unconquerable, but Joshua felt the Lord was with him, and he would be successful if he kept his faith in God. Joshua learned that the people of the city had become immoral because of their wealth and life of ease. He knew rumor and fear would spread like poison among them, so he planted seeds of rumor about the power of his army.

To invade Jericho was considered impossible. Joshua and the Israelites had faith in God. They did what God commanded. The walls of the "moon city" came tumbling down.

You and I are constantly being faced with tasks that would be impossible to do by ourselves. But, with God's help—what do you think?

FALLING ROCK

In Tallapoosa County, Alabama, a story is told about an Indian chief who had two sons. The twins were named Running Deer and Falling Rock.

The old chief loved the two boys equally, but he knew he must name one of them to be his successor. He sent them out to hunt, saying that the one who proved himself to be the better hunter would take his father's place. The sons were gone a long time before Running Deer finally returned. Truly his hunt had been successful.

Day after day passed, but Falling Rock did not come back to the camp. The father and brother and other members of the clan were deeply upset. They sent word to other tribes asking for any information they might have on the lost son. But there was no news. He never returned. The story says that today, if you are driving along a road in Tallapoosa County, you will see signs saying, "Look out for falling rock."

Jesus sent out his disciples to seek those who were falling away from that which is good. He told them to preach the gospel of repentance of sins. Most people remember their preaching but do not do much about repenting.

The ancient meaning of the word we translate as sin meant missing the mark. If a person with a bow and arrow let his eyes slip away from the target, he would miss the mark. It also referred to a person who crossed the starting line in a race before the beginning signal had been given. As Jesus used the word sin, he conveyed the meaning of a deliberate breaking of the law.

John the Baptizer was a cousin of Jesus. We believe that John belonged to a religious-political group called the

Essenes who had a private community south of Jerusalem on the shore of the Dead Sea. The Essenes were very conscious of wrongdoing. When they sinned, they would make public declaration of their determination to change their ways by taking a bath in front of the entire community. In other words, they rebaptized themselves. It was a way of saying they had departed from their misdoing.

John preached that all people must turn aside from evil and begin doing that which was right. He cried, "Repent." Jesus also said, "Repent." And he continued, "For the kingdom of God is at hand."

All of us, men and women, boys and girls, act like falling rocks, over and over again, falling away from the goodness of God. Jesus said we must not only be sorry for our misdoings but also stop falling.

SERENADE TO SPRING

"The flowers appear on the earth; the time of the singing of birds is come, and the voice of the turtle is heard in our land" (KJV).

Those words appear in the section of our Bible called the Song of Solomon. Some scholars believe they were part of a collection of folk songs recited at weddings and other celebrations, and some ancient editor included them in the Bible because he liked them.

What does it mean—the voice of the turtle? Would it make any difference to you if it read "the voice of the turtledove"? That is what it really meant. Why didn't the early translators say it that way in the King James Version of our Bible? No one knows.

The words are part of a wonderful ode, or serenade, to springtime. Modestly, the girl compares herself to a common flower. The fellow she is to marry turns what she has said into a compliment, comparing her to lovely lilies. Then, she likens him to an apple tree whose branches give cooling shade. He answers with another song of the charms of nature.

In Palestine there are really only two seasons of the year: one dry, the other wet. Winter is wet. When the turtledove arrives in Israel he coos sorrowfully, announcing that once again it is springtime. The boy, serenading beneath the window, says that his girl, who is hidden behind the window lattice, is like this lovely bird.

The Jewish festival of Passover comes in the springtime. It is the story of the escape of Jewish people from the bonds of slavery. As a salute to human freedom, it has given inspiration to countless millions for centuries. It speaks of a spring season in the life of a people.

Worldwide, there are customs and rites calling attention to spring, speaking of the resurgence of life. In Christian tradition, Easter, calling to mind the resurrection of Jesus, has become the center of spring celebrations.

Thorough housecleaning is a practice associated with the spring of the year. Christian women feel the need to have things spic and span in preparation for Easter. Jewish women want their homes to be sparkling clean for Passover. In Jewish tradition, they use the three days following what for Christians is Palm Sunday to do this thorough cleaning.

In the early days of Christianity, newly baptized Christians dressed in white linen clothing. As the years progressed, it became fashionable for the faithful to appear on Easter Sunday in new clothes, symbolizing new life. Until very recently the thing to do was walk down the street after the Easter church service to show off one's new clothing. It may be that this custom arose from long ago when people walked through fields and open spaces after Easter Mass.

Songs, rites, festivals, feasting and fasting, and Easter games are to be found in many places. They are like the voice of the turtledove that is heard in the land proclaiming, "God's in his heaven/All's right with the world!"

COUNT YOUR BLESSINGS

Jesus was a great storyteller. He was most skilled in the use of parables. A parable is a short story in which spiritual or moral truths are set forth. Matthew recalls a number of them for us. In one of these, Jesus talks about the "good guys."

To put it into today's way of speaking, Jesus said, "The good guy is one who, when he sees someone hungry will go out of his way to try to get him something to eat; for the thirsty, will provide water; when an individual has nowhere to go to get in out of the cold, he'll welcome him into his own home. But, the good guy is also the sort of person who doesn't take particular pride in what he's done, and responds, 'But, I can't remember when I saw you hungry, thirsty, or in need.' He or she is the kind of individual who will say, 'Listen, I only did what anyone else would have done if he had been in the same situation.' "

The question, of course, is, *Would* anyone else have done the things he did?

A man named Johnson Oatman, Jr., wrote a gospel song:

> When upon life's billows you are temptest-tossed,
> When you are discouraged, thinking all is lost,
> Count your many blessings, name them one by one,
> And it will surprise you what the Lord hath done.

We do not count our blessings often enough. We develop the habit of always looking on the dark side. Consider the little boy walking along the beach south of Pacifica, California. A wave knocked him down. He stood up. A second wave pushed him over. This time he could not regain his footing and was carried away out from shore. His mother shouted for help. A man ran into the water and rescued the boy. He said, "Everything is all right, lady."

The mother screamed back, "Everything's not all right! Where's his new hat?"

When were *you* hungry? When were *you* thirsty? When were *you* cold and had no shelter? We are talking about *you*. Almost every average boy or girl will have to answer, "Never." How often do you count your blessings?

The pilgrims suffered great hardships when they were settling America. The trip across the Atlantic from England on the *Mayflower* had been bad. There were storms. There wasn't proper protection or food. After they finally landed, they had to make shelters. Many were ill. Many died. When the winter was over, it took a lot of hard work to attempt to clear some land to plant seeds. There were many complaints.

In the fall, someone suggested it might be good to set aside a day on which they could recount their grievances and grumble to the Lord. However, some wise and courageous person suggested it would be better if they had the special day, not for gripes, but for saying thanks. They were alive, weren't they? They did have some shelter and some food, didn't they?

It must have been a hard idea for many of them to accept, but they did agree to it. Thanksgiving Day was born. It is a day when each of us should count our many blessings.

THE CROSS-EYED BEAR

Music included in a service of worship is usually either hymns, gospel songs, anthems, or a combination of two or more of them. As a rule, an anthem is sung by a choir, because a lot of practice is required to sing one properly. Formerly, an anthem was a hymn sung antiphonally, that is responsively. Now, it means a sacred choral composition that ordinarily has words from the Scriptures. An anthem can be very beautiful and inspiring.

Hymns and gospel songs are generally sung by a congregation. Most people do not realize the difference between hymns and gospel songs. Hymns are poems of praise, prayer, or adoration to God that have been set to music. Gospel songs are all personal, using the words "I" and "we." Generally, gospel songs have catchy tunes and a strong beat; and almost everyone, young and old, loves to really shout them out. They love the rhythm and the melody and disregard the words. If they thought about the words, they might not sing so lustily, like the one saying, "Oh, what a worm am I!"

There is an old story telling of a six-year-old who came home from Sunday school all excited. "Guess what," she said. "Today we sang about a cross-eyed bear!"

"Honey, I'm sure you're wrong. You certainly didn't sing of a cross-eyed bear."

"Honestly, Mommy, we did."

Puzzled, the mother telephoned the superintendent of the primary department. At first, the superintendent was equally bewildered. Then she began to laugh.

"Yes, one of the phrases in the song we taught the children this morning goes, 'Gladly, the cross I'd bear. "

When we are young, most of us feel intensely about everything. We are either extra happy or extra sad; way up on cloud nine or way down in the dumps. When we get older and begin to think back about our childhood events, we usually remember only those things that were happy and pleasant. Actually, childhood is no different from adulthood. There are sorrows and there are joys.

You are familiar with the story of how Jesus was forced to drag a heavy cross up a hill to the place where he was hung. Almost immediately after that, the cross became a symbol of problems and difficulties.

The apostle Paul occasionally referred to having problems of his own. We are not certain just what his troubles were. There have been many theories as to why he seemed to have felt ill a good deal of the time. He mentioned "the cross I bear" in referring to his difficulties. But none of this slowed him down in the task he felt God had called him to do. When we read about his many journeys, mostly on foot, we are astonished.

Dr. Kenneth Cooper, recognized as an authority on exercise, remarked that people do not die when exercising vigorously, but after they stop. You may have heard of people who have dropped dead after shoveling snow. Dr. Cooper says, "They go inside the house, sit down, and ask for a cup of tea or coffee, when what they should do is keep walking around and gradually slow down."

It is not the difficulty that gets us down, it is our attitude. Everyone has troubles. Everyone has crosses to bear. Some people get beaten down by their crosses. Others stand tall and march forward.

THE ANGELS' SONG

Phillips Brooks, one-time minister of Trinity Episcopal Church in Copley Square, Boston, Massachusetts, was deeply loved. He never married and had no children of his own, but he loved all children. Children also loved him. They seemed to be drawn to him as much as iron filings are pulled by a magnet. It was not only children who adored him. Adults loved him too and were inspired by him.

On Christmas Eve, 1865, Dr. Brooks was in Jerusalem. By horseback, he traveled to Bethlehem. Just as night was falling, he passed through the field where tradition tells us the shepherds were when they saw and heard the angels sing. The next morning he attended Mass at the Church of the Nativity, the building that stands above the cave where we are told Jesus was born.

Just after this event, Dr. Brooks wrote a lovely poem about Bethlehem. Later, his organist Lewis Redner set the words to music. As long as people sing, Dr. Brooks will be remembered for having written:

> O little town of Bethlehem,
> How still we see thee lie!
>   Above thy deep and dreamless sleep
>   The silent stars go by;
> Yet in thy dark street shineth
> The everlasting light;
>   The hopes and fears of all the years
>   Are met in thee tonight.

That child about whom the angels sang was the son of a couple from the town of Nazareth who had traveled to

Bethlehem to register for a census being conducted by the Roman authorities ruling that part of the world at the time.

It was evening when Mary and Joseph arrived in the town of Bethlehem. It was a cold night, and they were expecting the birth of a baby. Joseph told all this to an innkeeper. The man was interested and sympathetic, but he said, "I haven't any room in the caravansery, but I do have some nice straw out in the stable. You can bed down there, if you'd like."

The Bible says that about the same time, some shepherds were watching their sheep on the hillside, when suddenly the sky was filled with a crowd of angels singing, "Glory to God in the highest, and peace to men of good will." Their song told of a baby who would grow up and teach people how to live together, to praise God, and to love one another.

What was the result of this song? The shepherds went to seek Jesus. At first they were afraid, but being accustomed to seeing meteors in the sky, they soon lost their wonder and began to follow the beckoning star. A few of the shepherds had to remain with the sheep, so those who left and saw Jesus hurried back to tell them what had happened. They were the first missionaries.

When Dr. Brooks died, there were many, boys, girls, men, and women, who were saddened to have him leave this earthly life. Eloquent eulogies were spoken. But, no tribute surpassed the remark of one little girl, "Oh, how happy the angels must be!"

EXAMINATIONS

When Mary Ann Martin was in high school, she discovered she had the ability to cram for examinations. As she read, she seemed to photograph everything, so that when she took tests she could reread in her mind the exact details to get the correct answes. However, she also found that, after those examinations, she promptly forgot all she had learned. Her mind was empty, like a vacuum.

If you pick up a copy of *Who's Who in the World* and look up the name of Dr. A. William Loos, you will find a long paragraph on him and his accomplishments. In college, his close friends envied him. They said, "Bill never seems to need to crack a book. He knows everything."

One day, a professor said. "Mr. Loos, if you will wake up, I'll appreciate your answering my question." Much to the teacher's chagrin, Bill was able to respond correctly. His mind absorbs and retains anything he has seen, read, or heard. Yet, he is humble and kind in his relations with others. Although he is extremely brilliant, he does not consider himself better than anyone else.

What good are examinations in the cases of these two people? Mary Ann, because she was constantly being tested, concentrated on developing the capacity for retention. She is now a competent medical doctor. Dr. Loos realized his great gifts were from God and dedicated his life to dealing in international relations to promote world peace.

Quizzes, tests, midsemesters, finals—just to mention any of those words makes some young people twist and squirm and can give them headaches. If you do not have a photographic mind like Mary Ann, or remember everything like Dr. Loos, you need to study and memorize so you can pass exams. Yes, you can pray about it, but you have to work hard too. Remember the saying, "God helps those who help themselves."

Life is a school. Life can give you examinations. Probably neither you nor your parents know the names of Harold Dixon, Gene Aldrich, and Tony Pastula. But your grandparents undoubtedly remember that they were three fliers, the crew of a tiny bombing plane, who were adrift in a rubber boat for thirty-four days in the south Pacific Ocean. A book about their experiences entitled *The Raft* is available at the public library. If you read about the tests to which those fellows were submitted, you won't worry about school examinations.

The famous Bruce Jenner took an examination at the Olympics in Canada. He passed, and was given a gold medal. He worked hard for years to acquire his skills. But he had to have an examination to prove to himself and the world his great worth. Without this public test, he would never have known whether he had reached his goal in development. No one else would ever have been aware of his efforts, either.

A family from Indiana had driven the many miles of desert across Texas and Arizona, had entered California, gone across the border to Mexico and back again, and were west of Calexico before starting to climb a mountain that was about seven thousand feet high. The road seemed to run almost straight up. Their car and the family were tested. At last they reached Jacumba. It was late, but there was still some radiance from the sun lingering in the sky. Before they got into bed the moon had begun to shine brightly. In the morning, the hills were covered with a thin film of mist. The rising sun, coming up behind them, seemed to be trying to push them forward. Behind was the fascination and mystery of the past. Before them lay the allure of the future enshrouded in fog.

Examination of the past in the light of the strange conflicts of today may be considered the birth pains of a new age. Testing may not be fun, but without it, how are we going to know if we are ready for what lies ahead?

SUDDEN LIGHT

Not too long ago, when a people wanted to have chocolate pudding for dessert, they would put sugar, cocoa, flour, and salt in a saucepan; mix it well; then add beaten eggs and milk, and stir and stir as the mixture cooked over a fire. Then came the time when manufacturing companies made available packages in which the dry ingredients for a pudding were already mixed. All that needed to be done was pour the contents into a pan, add milk, and cook for a few minutes. Now, instant puddings are on the grocery shelves. Most of them still have to have milk added, but they do not require any cooking. They are ready to serve immediately.

Do you know what a conversion is? A conversion is a change in a person's moral and spiritual attitude in which he is so utterly and completely convinced about something he can hardly think or talk about anything else. A conversion can take a long, long time to come about, or it can happen as if in a sudden flash of light.

You remember that Paul was on his way from Jerusalem to Damascus to wipe out the Christians who were living there when he suddenly saw a bright light and heard a voice and had a conversion to follow Christ, to be a Christian himself. Paul made lots of trips and wrote lots of letters to promote Christianity. Many scholars feel that Paul's Letter to the Romans has had a greater influence on the thinking of modern people than any other writings except the four Gospels.

Martin Luther was born in Germany in 1483. He studied at the University of Erfurt and was second in his graduating class. We know he was an intelligent man. Just two months after beginning to study law, he renounced the world and entered an Augustinian monastery. He said this sudden change was due to a fear of death that came over him after he was knocked unconscious by a bolt of lightning.

Luther continued to study and received the degree of Doctor of Theology in 1512. He was sitting in his cell one day reading Paul's Letter to the Romans. Now, he had read this passage many times before, but this particular day as he repeated the sixteenth and seventeenth verses of the first chapter: "For I am not ashamed of the Gospel. It is the saving power of God for everyone who has faith. . . ." (NEB) there came another flash of lightning. From that moment, Luther became bold in his declarations of his faith in the power of Christ.

About a hundred and fifty years after the death of Martin Luther, a man named John Wesley was born in England. He attended Oxford University and became an ordained priest in the Church of England. He was attending a meeting in a church known as Aldersgate when he heard a man reading from Martin Luther's commentary on Paul's Letter to the Romans. Of that event, Wesley said, "I felt my heart strangely warmed. I felt I did trust in Christ, Christ alone, for salvation; and assurance was given me as though he had taken away my sins." Again there was a sudden change which seemed to come with the speed of lightning.

Words are powerful. All of us need to be careful what we say and write. As if with a flash of lightning words can destroy or build, break or make a life.

THE TOWER OF BABEL

Most of the major cities of the world have interesting museums. Days, weeks, even months might not be long enough to properly appreciate all the wonderful museums in Chicago, Illinois. The Museum of Science and Industry, the Chicago Historical, the Aquarium, the Planetarium, the little-known Huntington, and the Oriental Institute are all fascinating and instructional.

Among the exhibits at the Oriental Institute, which all have to do with the past history of humans, is a remarkable model of the Tower of Babel. The name *Babel* means "Gate of God" and referred to the city of Babylon, which had a tremendous influence on the life and thinking of the Children of Israel. It was a polyglot city. Its name became synonymous with confusion. In his translation of Genesis, Dr. Moffatt wrote, "Hence it was called Babylon, because it was there that the Eternal made a babble of the language of the whole earth."

One of the great problems facing our modern world is the diversity of languages. Many young people fuss at the idea of learning any language other than the one spoken in their own home. It is not that they are unable to learn to speak French, German, Japanese, Russian, or Spanish, but they do not want to put forth the effort. Often they do not even speak their own language properly.

At the time of the building of the Tower of Babel, people had little in the way of comforts. Many folks in the world today have few comforts. Many have insufficient food, clothing, and shelter. If we learn how to communicate with these unfortunate people, we may be able to help them overcome their handicaps. It is not possible to talk to them if we do not learn to speak their language. It would just be a babble of voices.

Stories of human accomplishment over the impossible are manifold. Early people learned how to use sticks and stones. They noted the usefulness of round stones and invented the wheel. They learned how to use water for power. They learned how to use fire.

We are in the process of leaning how to use the power of the atom without harming ourselves or future generations from the discarded waste materials. It may take a long time, but it can be done.

As you grow older, life may seem to babble for you a lot of the time. You may wonder if you can possibly solve all your problems. As you read history, you will find that other people, although they were often filled with doubts, accomplished much more than they thought they could.

You, too, can do much more than you think you can. You can bring order out of chaos.

THE LOOKING GLASS

There were two ancient Roman writers named Pliny, uncle and nephew, known as the elder and the younger. In his book *Natural History*, the elder suggested that glass mirrors were made by the Phoenicians before 1500 B.C.

How are glass mirrors made? By depositing a coating of silver, beryllium, or other metal on one side of a flat piece of glass. How thick a film is placed on the glass depends on the purpose for which the mirror is to be used.

When you were small, you learned to recite the old rhyme, "Mirror, mirror on the wall, who is the fairest of them all?" while looking into a mirror. But has it told you the truth? Mirrors can produce images that are not real and twist the appearance of whatever they show. When you look at yourself, the right side of your face appears on your right. If someone is looking at you, he sees your right side on his left.

Light rays striking a smooth surface behave like a billiard ball bouncing off the sides of a billiard table. The angle of the shot may be changed. In making a mirror, the glass surface must be so perfectly polished that there are no irregularities or the light will be refracted in such a way as to create distortions. Have you ever visited a hall of mirrors in an amusement park? Glass was bent in such a way that you appeared fat or tall, or both fat and tall.

Mirror images are optical illusions. Magicians and stage performers have used mirrors in tricks. A very old book, *Natural Magic*, by G. B. della Porta, told of actors performing behind inclined sheets of glass. The audience did not realize this. Other actors were concealed offstage, and their reflections were made to appear on stage as ghosts. The same method is used in motion pictures today to create ghosts.

Animals looking at themselves in a mirror cannot understand what they are seeing. Birds can be fooled into spending their whole lives in companionship with a reflection of themselves. Do you have a parakeet? Is a mirror in its cage?

Remember, when you are looking into a mirror you are seeing a reflection, not the real thing. Also, when you gaze into the looking glass, you are looking backward.

The apostle Paul wrote to the people of Corinth: "When I was a child, my speech, my outlook, and my thoughts were all childish. When I grew up, I had finished with childish things. Now we see only puzzling reflections in a mirror, but then we shall see face to face" (NEB).

BUILD MORE STATELY MANSIONS

Dr. Oliver Wendell Holmes lived in Boston, Massachusetts, but owned a summer home on the coast north of Boston at Beverly Farms in the area of Salem and Peabody. A group of wealthy people built homes in the town of Manchester, not far from Beverly Farms. Because they thought the name of their town too simple, they voted to change it to Manchester by the Sea. This amused Dr. Holmes. The leather factories of Peabody disposed of their used tanning solutions by dumping them into the North River. The river not only smelled, but on a warm night, it was overpowering. Dr. Holmes ordered some stationery for himself printed:

Oliver Wendell Holmes, M.D.
Beverly by the Smell

Dr. Holmes was an excellent physician, but he is particularly remembered because he was also a fine author. He wrote:

Build thee more stately mansions, O my soul,
   As the swift seasons roll!
      Leave thy low-vaulted past!
Let each new temple, nobler than the last,
   Shut thee from heaven with a dome more vast,
      Till thou at length art free,
Leaving thine outgrown shell by life's unresting sea!

The first written reference to the town of Oxford, England, is in a manuscript dated early in the tenth century entitled, "Anglo-Saxon Chronicle." Oxford was a frontier town, built at its particular location on the Thames River, not only because it had an easy river crossing, but also because it was well-protected on three sides by rivers and water meadows.

There have been many wars and revolutions during the years since the founding of the town, but fortunately, Oxford has never been touched by them. Architecturally, Oxford has always been alive. The town is considered one of the finest architectural monuments in the world, for it contains examples of every building style found in England from the eleventh century to the present. Each has been constructed with the idea of beauty and durability.

Beauty and durability are good foundations on which to build. You are just beginning to build your life. How are you going about it? What kind of foundations are you putting down? Pick up a copy of "The Chambered Nautilus," by Dr. Holmes, and become familiar with that fifth stanza of the poem which begins, "Build thee more stately mansions." Then, turn in your Bible to the twentieth chapter of Acts and read Paul's long speech to the elders at Ephesus, closing with, "I commend you to God and his gracious word which has power to build you up."

FORECASTING

From the moment of birth, you and I live in an ocean of air. This air is a mixture of gases: carbon dioxide, argon, nitrogen, oxygen, and others, which we call our atmosphere. Each gas with which we are surrounded performs a special duty. About fifteen miles above the earth is a layer of supercharged oxygen known as ozone. Its special task is to filter the light from the sun.

We are greatly affected by changes in the atmosphere and therefore want to know all we can about what is going to happen in the weather. The word *weather* covers a great deal: snow, rain, hail, drought, lightning, thunder. Weather, as we know it personally, takes place in a very small amount of atmosphere around us, but this air is conditioned by air in the troposphere just below the stratosphere.

At a very early time in our human existence, people recognized certain signs that were helpful in forecasting what might happen in the weather. A long, long time ago someone invented the rhyme:

> Evening red and morning grey
> Will speed a traveller on his way;
> But evening grey and morning red
> Will pour down rain upon his head.

The fact that air has weight came to be known in the early years of the seventeenth century when an Italian named Galileo Galilei realized that a pump could not draw water up in a pipe any higher than thirty-four feet. About the same time, another Italian physicist, and a friend of Galileo, Evangelista Torricelli, learned that mercury, which is more than thirteen times as heavy as water, would raise less than one-thirteenth as high as a column of water because of the pressure of the atmosphere. Thus, was born the barometer which, as you know, shows variations in atmospheric pressure.

It was Benjamin Franklin who has been credited with first noticing that storms move from place to place. He became aware that a storm he experienced in Philadelphia, Pennsylvania, traveled to Boston, Massachusetts, the following day. From this observation it was only a short jump to understand that other weather conditions also move from one place to another.

An international conference on weather was held in Vienna, Austria, in 1873. People had come to realize that weather paid no attention to national boundaries, and that by cooperation, they could help one another forecast the weather. One of the first weather stations specifically established to observe weather changes was set up in England.

The name *meteorology* comes from a Greek word meaning "higher than air." In 1919, the Meteorological Society of America was organized in Boston to study our atmosphere.

Not only can weather predictions be made, but sometimes weather conditions can be altered. On November 13, 1946, Dr. Vincent J. Schaefer went up in an aircraft and dropped dry ice crystals into a cloud. This produced a small snowstorm. Since then, many scientists have been doing other experiments, even trying to modify hurricanes.

Can you forecast your behavior? Perhaps you might if you would study yourself. Hardened criminals have been observed to try to discover what made them commit their crimes. Programs have been set up to help these criminals change their life-styles. Once it has been learned what triggers a criminal response, it may be possible to successfully rehabilitate these people.

It appears that, within a few years, we moderns can probably control our weather. However, we need to learn to control ourselves, too.

A MATTER OF THE HEAD

You have heard the expression, "Two heads are better than one."

Ed Paul is an American who likes to wear a kind of head covering called a beret. This type of hat is very popular in Europe but rather difficult to find in the United States. So, when he and his wife were visiting in the lovely city of Barcelona, Spain, Mr. Paul went into a hat store. He pointed to his beret. The Spaniard shook his head negatively and opened a drawer to show it was empty. On a piece of paper he drew a map indicating the location of another store. He escorted the Pauls to the door and pointed in the direction they should go. The new shop was not far. Again, Mr. Paul pointed to his head. The clerk pulled off the beret, measured around it with a tape, then placed a half dozen berets of the correct size on the counter and wrote down the cost. Mr. Paul picked out the one he preferred, counted out the Spanish money, and left completely satisfied. Two heads, each speaking a different language, had cooperated, with signs and smiles, to make a sale.

Level-headed is a complimentary adjective. To be level-headed is commendable. There are a number of uncomplimentary English terms using the word *head*: head-strong, big-headed, swell-headed, thick-headed, empty-headed, hard-headed, fat-headed. Each of these disliked characteristics need to be avoided. Each could be called proud-headed.

It is recorded that wise King Solomon said, "Pride goes before destruction, and a haughty spirit before a fall" (RSV). Pride can be a virtue or a vice. The difference is in attitude, humility or haughtiness. With humble pride, boys and girls will exert effort to grow and become better than they are, being unsatisfied with slipshod work. With haughty pride, boys and girls imagine themselves better than they actually are, they overvalue themselves. A girl named Jeannie Sue was gazing into a mirror. Her brother said, "You certainly think you're beautiful, don't you?" She retorted, "That's not true. I don't think I'm nearly as pretty as I am."

A proud Frenchman commissioned an artist to paint a picture for the banquet room of his mansion. It was the nobleman's version of Noah entering the ark. In his hand, Noah held a box on which was written: The deLevis Family Record.

Traveling by train between London and Bristol, England, you will see many small fields of beautiful wheat. In some fields the stalks stand strong and tall. If you were able to examine the heads closely, you would find them empty. They stand for the vice of haughty pride. In nearby fields, the grain is bent over almost touching the grounds. If you were able to inspect it, you would find it heavy with nourishing seeds. It is the symbol of the virtue of humble pride.

WHO OWNS IT?

As they are parting, many people say, "Have a nice day!" Those are pleasant words if spoken in earnest, but if they are merely a routine statement they are meaningless. Store clerks have been known to say them to customers at nine at night when the day is really gone.

Some years ago, a college professor would greet his students with "How's your day?" It was his trademark, such a standard question that his students disregarded it.

Whose day is it? Is it *yours* as the professor suggested? Not really. The day belongs to God. Like everything else we enjoy, it has been loaned to us by our Heavenly Father. To some people he lends a great many days. To others he gives only a very few. People do not know how many days have been allowed to them.

Some mornings when you wake, the sun is shining brightly. You run to the kitchen, happy as a lark. The smell of bacon penetrates every corner of your being. Even though you do not want to drink coffee, the aroma is a pleasant stimulus to make you wide awake. After breakfast you run outside to play. All of a sudden a cloud appears in your sky. You remember the nasty remark your pal Jerry made about you yesterday. It was bad enough he said it, but humiliating that the other boys and girls heard him. Your anger returns. Your bright day has become gloomy even though the sun is still shining and the flowers are a rainbow of colors. Back into the house you go and begin making everyone else as miserable as you are.

Jesus told the story of a man who had three servants. He explained to them that he was going away on a business trip and they would be in charge while he was gone. He gave each of them cash: one received one thousand dollars, another two thousand dollars, and the third five thousand dollars. When he returned, he called the man who had been given five thousand dollars. This servant had invested the money and doubled it. The master said, "Good, you've done well with that small amount, I'll make you in charge of more." The man who had been given two thousand dollars also had doubled his amount and was commended. The one who had been given one thousand dollars told of burying the money for safekeeping. The master was very angry and took the money from him saying, "You ought to have invested my money so I could have received interest."

All days are waiting to be developed, full of potential. You can fill them with the sunshine of good work and good works or you can remember the nasty remark made to you and waste the day in feeling miserable. The story Jesus told admonishes us to make wise use of what has been given to us. Time is one of the most precious of God's gifts. We need to value each day and make the best possible use of it.

A wise man once wrote: "What is time? The shadow on the dial, the striking of the clock, the running of the sand, day and night, summer and winter, months, years, centuries . . . those are but the arbitrary and outward signs. The measure of time, not time itself. Time is the life of the soul."

PROPELLERS

Take two identical pieces of wood, lay them side by side, then drive a wood screw through them. What happens? The screw draws one piece to the other. This is the same principle we find in the propeller that pushes a ship through the water or an airplane through the air. Turning in one direction, the screw pulls. In the other, it pushes.

In the southeast of England is a region known as Romney Marsh. It was there that Francis Pettit Smith was born, raised, and began his work as a grazing farmer. His hobby was building model boats. Today, most boys and girls who build model boats use kits. But kits were not available in those days. Francis whittled and carved a piece of hardwood, preferably oak, to make his miniatures. Mr. Smith moved to a farm at Hendon, which is now part of the city of London. He had an idea he might drive one of his boats with a propeller. It may have seemed a silly idea, but he could not get it out of his head. He experimented and finally fashioned a propeller out of wood and fixed it to a shaft at the stern of one of his models. He tried out the boat successfully on a small pond on his farm. Then he obtained a patent for his invention, and determined to try the idea on a full-sized boat. That venture was not successful. The wooden propeller broke. Modern propellers are made from metals, such as nickel, aluminum, and bronze.

The word "propel" means to drive onward, to push ahead. The propeller does the driving, the pushing. Deep in the hull of a ship is the engine room. There, powerful engines turn the propeller, which sucks the water from the front and forces it out behind, moving the ship forward. Most propellers have from two to seven blades. Racing craft have only two. Ocean-going vessels have more blades in order to cut down on vibration.

Proverbs lists the best sayings of wise men from earliest times. They are thought-propellers. Paul wrote many letters to churches in various parts of the Roman world. The things he said are good-thought propellers. The books of Matthew, Mark, Luke, and John are filled with the sayings of Jesus. His teachings can propel you through life. Follow them!

TWO BOARDS AT A TIME

W. J. Wilmont Buxton said, "To do anything great requires time, patience, and perseverance."

The early settlers of the territory of what came to be known as New Hampshire were rugged folks. Ethan Allen Crawford was one of the most interesting of this hardy group. He stood almost seven feet tall and was called the Giant of the Hills. Today, there are many who reach that height, but in those days it was unusual. Until he was thirteen, he never owned or wore shoes or mittens. He learned to be tough.

The Crawfords, Ethan, his brother Thomas, and their father, were fascinated by Mount Washington, 6,288 feet, the highest mountain not only in New Hamshire but also in the entire eastern part of the United States. In 1819, Ethan and his father blazed a trail to the top of Mount Washington. It took a lot of hard work and perseverance. A year later, Thomas improved the trail enough so that he and Ethan were able to take a party of men from Lancaster to the summit. On horseback, they rode to the area known as the Giant's Grave, then continued on foot. When they reached the top, they began to sing, "O, be joyful unto the Lord." They talked about the beauty around them and how close they felt to God.

The weather on Mount Washington is said to be the worst in the United States. An official weather station at the summit is snowed in or buffeted by gale winds much of the year. The trip up had been difficult for Ethan, Tom, and the others, but not nearly as hard an experience as going down. One man dropped to the ground, exhausted. He weighed over two hundred pounds, but Ethan picked him up and carried him the rest of the way.

It was Ethan who acted as guide for the first girls who climbed to the mountaintop.They were three sisters from Portsmouth, named Austin. The girls thought the view was good payment for their hard work and perseverance. Their enthusiasm made others eager to climb.

In 1852, three residents of Lancaster decided it would be a good business venture to have a hotel atop the mountain and raised money for the project. The lumber for constructing Summit House was carried up the mountain on a horse, one board fastened on each side. In order that the lumber would not drag on the ground, two men followed the horse, each holding up the end of a board. Today the project would have been finished in a short time. Probably helicopters would have lifted the building material from a base camp. But, whether you use two boards on a horse or modern technology, to accomplish a task you need perseverance.

A number of years ago, an Englishman made a model of one of his country's famous cathedrals. It attracted a lot of attention. Why? Because the building material he used was discarded corks he had picked up along the streets. A printed card beside the model carried the words:

> Nothing but perseverance, corks, and glue.
> Made in eighteen hundred sixty-two.

HOW IT STARTED

Wars or famines in their countries have forced people to flee to other lands. There have been many recent stories of refugees from Vietnam and Cambodia, but the refugee situation is not a new one. The United States was founded by refugees, and during the years since that time, its doors have been open to thousands more.

A long time ago, Jacob and his family lived in Palestine. Everyone worked hard and prospered until a drought came. Winds settled thick dust on young plants, smothering them. Without crops, people were hungry. Jacob sent his sons to Egypt to search for food. They were welcomed into the new land. They thought it would be a good place so they married and settled there.

The pharaoh at that time was a good ruler, but when he died he was succeeded by a cruel king who made slaves of Jacob's family. The slave population was growing. The pharaoh feared an uprising, so he ordered that newborn Jewish boy babies be killed. In order to save her little son, a mother made a basket of reeds, covered it with pitch, and hid it in the shallow waters on the riverside. You remember the story of the king's daughter finding the baby Moses and raising him as her own.

One day when Moses was older, he was watching the slaves tramping straw into wet clay to be used as a binder in making bricks. It was hot, difficult work. Moses saw an Egyptian officer strike a slave. He was furious. Moses knew he belonged to the same tribe as the slave working on the building project, but because he had been found by the king's daughter he was living in luxury. He killed the officer and escaped into the land of the Midianites. There, he tended sheep. One day, Moses saw a flaming bush and heard the voice of God telling him to lead the slaves out of Egypt so they could be free. Moses was to tell the pharaoh, "Let my people go!"

Now there was a new pharaoh. He promised to free the slaves but, over and over again, at the last minute changed his mind. The Lord was angry. He told Moses to order each Jewish family to kill a lamb on a particular evening and to put some of the animal's blood on the two doorposts and the lintels of their homes. The Lord said he would go through the land and all the first-born Egyptian people and animals would die, but he would pass over the houses marked with blood. From that time to the present, Jewish people have observed that event as a time of memorial called Passover.

Jesus and his disciples met in an upper room in Jerusalem to observe the Passover Feast. As they were eating, Jesus took some bread, blessed it, and told his disciples to eat. He did the same with the wine. He told them it was the last meal they would have together. Christians continue to celebrate that Passover meal, calling it the Last Supper, Holy Communion, Mass, the Eucharist. It is a time for all who follow Jesus to listen to the voice of God, to commune with him.

THE FESTIVAL OF LIGHTS

Drew is a Christian who is attending a very fine Jewish day school because it is better than the public school in his area. His grandfather lives far away in another state, but telephones him every Saturday. One day late in November the grandfather asked, "What have you been doing, Drew?" expecting the six-year-old to talk about preparation for Christmas. Drew replied, "I'm having lots of fun. I'm getting ready for Hanukkah!" This is a Jewish celebration that comes around Christmas each year.

Over three hundred years before the birth of Jesus, a young man became king of Macedonia. He was one of the most brilliant men in his era, a military expert who conquered a lot of territory. Into his new lands the ruler introduced the Greek culture and way of life. His name was Alexander. The world calls him Alexander the Great.

After he died, his empire was divided into several provinces, each ruled by a general. The largest area was given to Seleucus. It was one of the Seleucid successors who conquered Palestine about two hundred years before Jesus was born.

Greek culture influenced many Jews. They admired the Greek poet Homer and the philosophers Plato and Aristotle. They appreciated the beautiful Greek temples, sculptures, and paintings. Antiochus IV came into power. This man we call Epiphanes tried to destroy Judaism completely. He prohibited Jewish religious observances and demanded that Jews worship Greek gods. He used the Temple at Jerusalem as a shrine to Zeus and ordered pigs to be sacrificed on the altar. This was a nasty thing to do.

The high priest named Mattathias refused to obey the

order. He and his sons fled to the hills, were joined by many others, and began fighting for religious freedom. After the death of the high priest, his son, Judas Maccabaeus became leader and defeated the army, entered Jerusalem, and retook the Temple.

In Judaism, the number seven is a symbol for natural order: seven days in a week. The number eight, being one number above the natural order, is a symbol for the eternity of God, the eternity of Truth, and of people transcending their earthly existence. The menorah is a candlestick with nine cups for holding candles, or nine orifices for burning oil. The center cup or orifice serves as the source for lighting the others. When Judas Maccabaeus and his followers entered the Temple they found only enough sacred oil for lighting the menorah one night. By a miracle, the oil kept burning for the entire eight-day rededication period.

The commemorative celebration may be referred to in several ways: Feast of the Maccabees, which is self-explanatory; Feast of Rededication, or Feast of Chanukah, to give it the Hebrew name. A third term is Feast of Lights, which brings to mind the miracle of the oil that kept providing light beyond its ability.

It is good to remember those who fought for freedom and justice. It is wise to celebrate worthwhile events.

GREAT BALLS OF FIRE

The Feast of Weeks was so named from Shabuoth, the Hebrew word meaning weeks. Each Jewish person was supposed to count the days of the seven weeks between Passover and Shabuoth eagerly. On the fiftieth day they were to take the first fruits of their orchards and fields to the Temple as an offering. Greeks gave this celebration the name Pentecost, from the Greek word *pentekoste* meaning fiftieth.

It was for this celebration that the disciples were gathered together after Jesus' death. In the second chapter of Acts, Luke tells us, "Suddenly a sound came from heaven like the rush of a mighty wind, and it filled all the house where they were sitting. And there appeared to them tongues as of fire, distributed and resting on each one of them. And they were all filled with the Holy Spirit" (RSV).

That all happened a long time ago. How could it possibly be true? Somebody told a tall tale. Did he? Here are three modern-time, true stories of incidents of mighty winds, lights, and balls of fire similar to those biblical tongues of fire.

In September late in the nineteenth century, Mrs. William Woody and her daughters, Elizabeth and Florence, were sitting in front of their kitchen fireplace in Bristol, England. They were preparing fruit for puddings to be steamed the next day, so they would be cured in time for Christmas. What appeared to be a ball of fire came down the chimney, rolled across the floor, under Mrs. Woody's chair, circled the room and went out through a window without harming the glass. The three were not hurt in any way, but they were covered with black soot, which had come down the chimney with the fireball.

During March in the 1960s, a tornado struck Louisville, Kentucky. Balls of fire about the size of oranges rolled along telephone wires, around cornices of buildings, and about the streets. Many of them exploded with loud crashes.

In October during the 1950s, a family living in Maracaibo, Venezuela, were awakened by a humming noise. The house appeared to vibrate with the sound. Then, a bright light filled the entire house. The family believed the world had come to an end. Worse than the light, there was a sound like vomiting, so severe that all nine family members felt ill. Next morning, there were swollen places on their bodies. A few days later their hair fell out, but none of them were severely injured. It was not long until the leaves of the trees around the house turned brown and fell to the ground.

What happened to the disciples? Was it a "tall" story? Or was it real? There is no positive proof either way. All we know is that something happened to the disciples and they believed Jesus had kept his promise and had sent them the Holy Spirit. They were changed men.

LOVE YOURSELF

A common practice of those who did not like Jesus or were afraid of him was asking him questions, trying to trick him. One lawyer asked, "Teacher, what is the greatest commandment?"

Jesus replied, "You shall love the Lord your God with all your heart, and with all your soul, and with all your mind. This is the great and first commandment. And a second is like it. You shall love your neighbor as yourself" (RSV).

People usually quote only the first part: *love your neighbor* and omit *as yourself*. But those two words should not be left out, because we cannot possibly love our neighbors unless we first love ourselves.

Janice lives in Port Elizabeth, South Africa. She is a pleasant girl but has a very low opinion of herself and her ability. She never misses an opportunity to downgrade herself. She recognizes nothing worthwhile in others, either. She thinks her brother Don is loud and their neighbor Betty a show-off. Until Janice begins to value herself as the desirable, clever girl she actually is, there is no chance whatsoever that she will be able to appreciate any good qualities in Don, Betty, or anyone else.

Lois was born in Illinois. She is not good-looking. She certainly does not have a good figure, in fact, she's dumpy. She thought she could sing. Her parents tried to discourage her, saying there had never been a singer in the family. But Lois had confidence in herself. She sang. People liked her voice. She now supports herself by singing. When Lois walks into a room, somehow all attention focuses on her, not because she has become well-known, but because of her faith in herself. She seems to have the power to make others feel at ease. She gives each person her undivided attention, her understanding. She loves people and they, in turn, love her.

Plato, the great Greek philosopher told his students, "Know thyself." Jesus admonishes us, "Love your neighbor *as yourself.*"

BE ALERT

Miss Robinson was talking to her pupils in the seventh grade at Washburn School, "You must be alert."

Jean whispered to Meg, "What's a lert?" The girls giggled.

"Tell the rest of us what's funny. We want to enjoy it too."

So Jean told the class. The teacher smiled, "That's a good question, but we all know there's no such noun as *lert*, and that I was using the adjective *alert*. That word has been in our language a long time. At first it referred to something held up so that all could see it. Later, it came to mean wide awake or on the lookout. To be "on alert" was used concerning soldiers on watch. When I say, "Be alert," I'm suggesting that you pay strict attention, that you be vigilant.

There is a type of caterpillar called the processionary worm. Why that name? Because several of them walk in a single file, one following another. A man was watching a line of them one day. As an experiment, he picked up two from the line and placed them at the very end. Seeing the gap left by the removal of the two, others hurried and closed up the space. They were alert.

In the spring of 1979, at a junior high school in Sumiton, Alabama, an eighth-grade student was helping the school custodian stock a soft drink machine. While removing cases of pop from the storage room, the boy noticed a box filled with white pills. He took some, put them in his pocket, and later gave some to a sixth-grade pupil. The younger boy passed his out to some friends. Some of them swallowed the pills. When others became aware the pills they were handling were causing a burning sensation, they told their teachers. It was discovered those pills were potassium hydroxide tablets, stored for use in science class. Antidotes were given to those who had swallowed the pills, and about twenty were treated for caustic burns. Some had to remain in the hospital several days for observation. Fortunately no one died because of the incident, but no one would have been poisoned or burned if they had been alert.

The apostle Peter wrote, "Be vigilant."

WHAT DO YOU HEAR?

George was brought up on a small farm just north of Kokomo, Indiana. One summer he went to visit his cousin Frank in Chicago. The big city was a surprise to George. He was not sure he liked it. Frank lived in an apartment near the Museum of Science and Industry. George was thrilled with the many interesting displays, and the cousins spent day after day there.

After a while though, George tired of this kind of sight-seeing. He wanted the feel of grass under his feet. The boys began to wander around the park that surrounds the museum. All of a sudden George said, "Stop a minute. I hear a cricket."

Frank answered, "You're crazy. You can't possibly hear a cricket."

"Yes, I do." George got down on his knees and turned left and right trying to focus his ears on the sound. Sure enough, beside the roots of a bush, there was the cricket.

Frank was astonished. "I couldn't hear that cricket. All I heard was the noise of the city."

Jesus said, "He who has ears to hear, let him hear."

What do you hear? Do you hear gossip, the nasty things others are saying about you or your friends? Or do you hear all the good, kind comments, the compliments?

In the play *Saint Joan*, by George Bernard Shaw, the King of France questions Joan d'Arc about the voices she hears. "Why don't they speak to me?" Her reply was, "They do!"

A minister was saying things in his sermon one morning that he knew would not be popular with some of the members of his church. As people were leaving after the service, one elderly gentleman, pointing to his hearing aid, remarked, "I shut the darn thing off." Do we sometimes shut off our ears when someone tries to correct us, or when we are told not to do something we want and plan to do? Yes. Young and old, we are all guilty. We hear only those things we want to hear.

Frederick William Faber said, "There is hardly ever a complete silence in our soul. God is whispering to us well-nigh incessantly. Whenever the sounds of the world die out in the soul, or sink low, then we hear these whisperings of God."

SPIRITUAL BREATHING

Alfred Lord Tennyson, was one of England's greatest poets. In "Morte D'Arthur," the story of the death of King Arthur, he wrote: "More things are wrought by prayer than this world dreams of."

Prayer is one of the strongest and least understood powers God has given us. Interesting and amazing studies have been conducted in Russia and in the United States with regard to extrasensory perception, those powers that seem to be within us with which we are able to reach out beyond our physical bodies. Some people have greater powers of ESP than others. It has been learned that people can develop their extrasensory abilities to a higher degree if they concentrate and practice. So it is with prayer, our spiritual communication with God. We need to concentrate and practice the art of praying.

Edward Vernon Rickenbacker was an outstanding air ace in World War I. During World War II, the United States government sent him on an inspection trip to the Far East. He and seven others were forced down in the Pacific Ocean and adrift for twenty-four days before being rescued. Captain Eddy wrote a book on those experiences, which tells some astonishing stories about prayer. It is well worth reading.

Charley lived in Marblehead, Massachusetts. He owned a boat, not a large one, but a very nice one. He, his brother, and a friend went out beyond Mystery Island in it. About dusk, as they were homeward bound, the engine began to sputter. Then it stopped completely. They tried to fix it, but were unable to do so. There was no other boat in sight, and they had no CB or ship-to-shore radio, so they were helpless. They were drifting in an easterly direction, in other words, out to sea. They began to panic. Out of the blue, one of the boys said, "Fear not, for I am with you always." He shook his head. "Don't know why I said that, it just came to me. Haven't heard those words since my early days in church school. Maybe it means we should start to pray." That is exactly what they did. You might say what happened was just by chance or coincidence, but you would never persuade those three that it wasn't prayer that led them to float to the west, so that by daylight they were only a short distance out from shore.

Over the years our English language has changed a great deal. Some words have come to have meanings different from the original. That is why we continue to have new versions of the Bible, to put words into the vernacular. One word that has changed dramatically is "comfortable." Today it means a sense of being at ease. It was derived from two Latin words con meaning "with" and fortis meaning "strong" or "strength." So, when Isaiah cried to God, "Comfort you, my people," he was not praying for God to give the people an easy life, but strength to meet their difficulties.

An oriental Christian, Sadhu Sundar Singh, once told a group that when he had been sitting by a river, he saw fish come to the surface as if to breathe. When he inquired about it, he was told the fish could not live all the time at the bottom of the stream. He declared, "The soul also needs to breathe. Prayer is spiritual breathing."

THE GREAT GARNET

Indians who lived in the White Mountains of New Hampshire told about vast treasures of precious stones that were in the "Crystal Hills." White men also claimed that jewels were hanging everywhere and that they were free for the taking. A man named Darby Field spoke of diamonds and emeralds that blazed and flashed, beckoning to be seized.

It was also said that Indians had hidden a great garnet, more precious than any ruby, somewhere in the mountains, and an evil spirit was standing guard over it. An early writer said this enormous stone was suspended from a crag, overlooking a dark lake, and could be seen from a great distance at night, glowing like a hot coal.

Indians declared that no mortal could hope to grasp this huge firestone, for it was guarded by the spirit of the mountains. If the spirit saw humans approaching, it would agitate the lake waters, causing a dark mist to rise, and those who came to steal it would be killed. It was a strong warning, but it was ignored. Many people went searching. They hoped to get "something for nothing."

Marcie was a lucky girl. She was given an opportunity to become a junior clerk at Penney's. She was told she would be moved from one department to another; that if she did a good job, she would have a regular position, perhaps be trained as a buyer, when she graduated from high school. One day Marcie showed her friend Kim a pretty new bracelet. She explained, "It was on the floor in the jewelry section, so I picked it up and put it in my pocket. They will never miss it. Even if they do, the store has insurance to cover it." Did Marcie get something for nothing? At the time she thought she had. When she was fired because of the incident, she knew she hadn't.

Can anyone ever get something for nothing? Yes, there are some things that do not cost us anything, God's love and protection. They are absolutely free. They are worth more than any expensive jewels, more than that great garnet hanging in the hills.